THE NEW ILLUSTRATED GUIDE TO

MODERN
AIRCRAFT
MARKINGS

SMITHMARK

THE NEW ILLUSTRATED GUIDE TO

MODERN
AIRCRAFT
MARKINGS

MIKE SPICK & BARRY WHEELER

A Salamander Book

©Salamander Books Ltd.

This edition published in 1992 by
SMITHMARK Publishers, Inc.,
16 East 32nd Street, New York,
NY 10016,
(212) 532 6600.

ISBN 0-8317-5058-8

Credits

Authors: Barry Wheeler is a writer and defense journalist who is currently the editor of *Air International* magazine. Mike Spick is a freelance writer who specialises in aviation subjects.

Editors: Graham Smith, Bob Munro
Designers: Mark Holt and Stonecastle Graphics
Filmset by: The Old Mill, London.
Color Reproduction: by Scantrans PTE, Singapore.
Printed in Hong Kong

Acknowledgements

The publishers wish to thank the many individuals, especially those in the US government, armed services and aerospace industry who have helped with the provision of photographs for this book.

Contents

Introduction

'Solve the problem of canopy glint and you could earn a fortune' observed a British camouflage expert wryly. No matter how effective aircraft camouflage is, the merest reflection from a cockpit canopy can compromise its concealment and give away the machine's position possibly to an enemy pilot and with likely fatal results.

For centuries, colour and insignia have been associated with military forces. In ancient times Roman legions raised their own distinguishing standard to indicate their position, while in China armies divided into units, each carrying a different plain-coloured flag, and the advent of armour in the Middle Ages and the widespread use of helmets that hid the faces of the wearers led to the adoption of brightly-coloured surcoats and shields for identification. British Army regiments took up the use of the standard known as the Colours and these were symbolic of the very spirit of the regiment being carried into battle in the centre of the line, always closely guarded; where they stopped, there the regiment stood, and if necessary the last man would defend the Colours to the death. To lose the Colours was the ultimate disgrace.

The arrival of the aeroplane early in this century called for some kind of distinguishing mark to indicate its operator and nationality. Although the flags were flown from airships, it was not aerodynamically practical to display them from aircraft, so the national emblem was painted on the wings, tails and/or fuselages of early machines. Military markings for aircraft were agreed under the Hague Convention 1907, while the registration of civilian aircraft was instituted internationally in 1919 by the Paris Air Convention.

Current national insignia generally relate to national flags and designs vary considerably. Colours also correspond in most cases to the national emblem, though there is a growing trend to reduce or eliminate altogether brightness in combat aircraft

markings. In their place pastel shades are being applied and in some cases only outlines of the original markings are carried. A state of tension between countries or even open conflict will result in national insignia being reduced in size or possibly removed completely, which is fine if you have air superiority or an effective IFF (identification friend or foe) system: if not, mis-identification can lead to aircraft being shot down by friendly forces.

All markings carried by modern combat aircraft have a role to play, from the smallest 'no step' which prevents personnel unfamiliar with the machine from damaging parts of the airframe, to large tail codes which identify units and sometimes bases. A diminishing number of markings are now applied to Western front-line machines, which reduces costs but is a cause of frustration to the large number of enthusiasts world-wide who follow this subject. In fact they have not been served too

Above: Reflection bouncing off the engine intakes and canopy of a US Navy F-14A Tomcat prior to the application of matt paint.

Below: Official specification for RAF roundels. The diameter (D) varies according to the size of the aircraft.

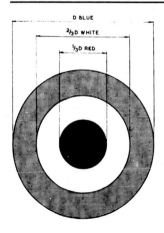

D BLUE
²/₃D WHITE
¹/₃D RED

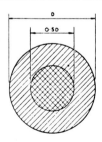

D
0.5D

ROUNDEL BLUE
B.S.381C/110

POST OFFICE RED
B.S.381C/538

KEY

ROUNDELS-STANDARD

ROUNDELS-CAMOUFLAGED AIRCRAFT

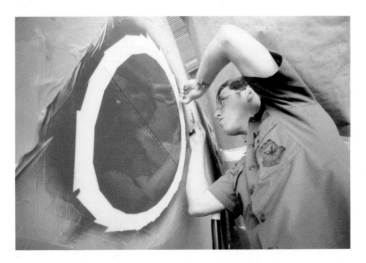

Above: One way of doing it.
Tech Sgt Ronald Breeman
removes the masking on a
Japanese F-15 following the
application of the national
marking. While the majority of
large insignia are sprayed on, an
increasing number are applied as
self-adhesive transfers.

**Below: One of many official US
schemes applied to F-5Es.**

**Right: During trials to determine
the most effective tactics to be
used by USAF A-10A
Thunderbolts, a series of
camouflage schemes were
evaluated by the 57th TTW in
November 1977. This mottled
scheme was applied to every
part of the aircraft and was
changed from day to day to
match weather and terrain
conditions.**

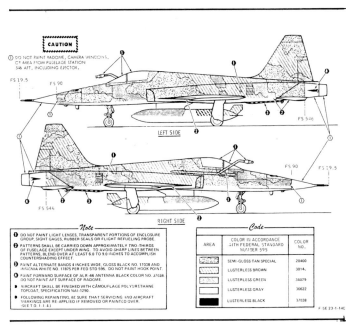

CAUTION

① DO NOT PAINT RADOME, CAMERA WINDOWS,
Cº AREA FROM FUSELAGE STATION
546 AFT, INCLUDING EJECTOR.

FS 19.5   FS 90

LEFT SIDE   FS 546

FS 90   FS 19.5

FS 546   RIGHT SIDE

Note

❶ DO NOT PAINT LIGHT LENSES, TRANSPARENT PORTIONS OF ENCLOSURE
GROUP, SIGHT GAGES, RUBBER SEALS OR FLIGHT REFUELING PROBE.

❷ PATTERNS SHALL BE CARRIED DOWN APPROXIMATELY TWO-THIRDS
OF FUSELAGE EXCEPT UNDER WING. TO AVOID SHARP LINES BETWEEN
PATTERNS, BLEND OVER AT LEAST 6.0 TO 9.0 INCHES TO ACCOMPLISH
COUNTERSHADING EFFECT.

❸ PAINT ALTERNATE BANDS 4 INCHES WIDE, GLOSS BLACK NO. 17038 AND
INSIGNIA WHITE NO. 17875 PER FED STD 595. DO NOT PAINT HOOK POINT.

❹ PAINT FORWARD SURFACE OF ALR-46 ANTENNA BLACK COLOR NO. 37038.
DO NOT PAINT AFT SURFACE OF RADOME.

❺ AIRCRAFT SHALL BE FINISHED WITH CAMOUFLAGE POLYURETHANE
TOPCOAT, SPECIFICATION NAI-1290.

❻ FOLLOWING REPAINTING, BE SURE THAT SERVICING AND AIRCRAFT
MARKINGS ARE RE-APPLIED IF REMOVED OR PAINTED OVER.
(SEE T.O. 1-1-4.)

Code

AREA	COLOR IN ACCORDANCE WITH FEDERAL STANDARD NUMBER 595	COLOR NO.
	SEMI-GLOSS TAN SPECIAL	20400
	LUSTERLESS BROWN	3014L
	LUSTERLESS GREEN	34079
	LUSTERLESS GRAY	36622
	LUSTERLESS BLACK	37038

F 5E 23-1-14C

well in recent years. Not only have markings faded, but the aircraft that carry them have gone to ground — or, more correctly, many front-line machines have been positioned in hardened aircraft shelters (HAS) throughout Europe, to lessen the chances of destruction from a surprise attack. Consequently, a look across a military airfield today will generally produce a scene barren of combat aircraft, but covered with small camouflaged hangarettes in which the warplanes sit armed and ready. It should be mentioned that

the Eastern Bloc also adopted this idea, although the freedom to walk up to the fence of a Warsaw Pact base until recently was denied to all but the foolhardy.

Hand in hand with the general toning down of markings is the use of dull but practical camouflage colours: the Vietnam war put paid to the polished metal finishes of the 1950s and 1960s and drab disruptive schemes took over. Initially greens and browns dominated the scene, but in recent years fighters have donned greys in what has become

known as counter-shading of very similar colours. Whereas the use of grey can be traced back to its application by the Luftwaffe during World War II, the new colours are subtle and amazingly effective. Evolved by a process of experimentation, the latest schemes can be considered the very best in low-visibility camouflage. However, they must also be able to withstand the constant attention of maintenance crews and be weather resistant. The paint manufacturers are constantly striving for better products and to meet new requirements from the air forces such as radar-absorbent paint. For aircraft not designed for 'stealth'

operations, the next best thing is to cover them with a material which will absorb the radar signals and reduce their signature and therefore their liability to detection.

This book considers only the combat aircraft in current service with the world's air forces, although where applicable other types are noted in the context of front-line use. Throughout the text, references to British colours are related to the British Standard series BS381C and BS4800 followed by the individual number. The equivalent American series are known as Federal Standard No 595a Colours. Each five-figure reference number for the actual col-

our has an initial digit which indicates whether it is (1) glossy, (2) semigloss or (3) lustreless (or matt). The second digit indicates the selected colour classification group, while the last three figures indicate the approximate order of increasing (diffuse) reflectance and are assigned nonconsecutively to leave gaps for future additions.

Model-makers should find these references useful, although no attempt has been made to match them to the various specialized model paint ranges as this book is not intended as a modelling guide. Nothing remains static for very long and colour schemes and markings

Above: Don't be fooled by the bright colours carried by modern service aerobatic team aircraft. Most have a war role, as shown by this Italian Air Force MB.339PAN of the *Frecce Tricolori,* equipped with pod-mounted cannon and iron bombs. Fifteen have been delivered to the team.

constantly change, sometimes imperceptibly and at others quite markedly. The name of the game is to improve aircrew and aircraft survivability and, with this in mind, the subject of colours and insignia will always hold a fascination.

15

National Insignia

Afghanistan

The present Afghan Republican Air Force insignia was adopted following the Soviet intervention of December 1979, replacing a triangular marking comprising the traditional Mohammedan colours of red, green and black in segmented form. In this insignia, the central star represents

Albania

Due to the secretive nature of the country's Communist regime, photographs of combat aircraft operated by the Albanian People's Army Air Force are almost non-existent, and those that have been released show few points of interest regarding markings. The force's

Algeria

This former French colony has an air arm equipped largely with aircraft of Soviet origin, particularly in the front-line combat squadrons. Known as Al Quwwat Aljawwiya Aljza'eriiya, the Algerian Air Force has about 36 MiG-25 'Foxbat' interceptor and reconnaissance aircraft supported by 80 MiG-21 'Fishbed's, while ground-attack equipment includes MiG-23 'Flogger's and Su-7 and Su-20 'Fitter's, plus some ageing MiG-17 'Fresco's. These and other aircraft in service carry the national marking, formed by the colours of Islam, on wings and fuselage. A flash is also normally applied on the fin, and three-digit numbers, often in arabic form, are painted on the nose to indicate the individual aircraft in the squadron. Transport and other types have a call-sign prefixed 7T, examples being 7T-WFT, a Potez Magister, and 7T-WHY, applied to one of 16 Lockheed C-130 Hercules bought by the Air Force.

the current socialist government. Most ARAF combat aircraft (MiG-21s, MiG-23s, Su-7s and Su-20/22s) carry the symbol on the fins and wings, and have a three-digit identification number each side of the nose. Early MiG-17s were given a two-number code on the nose, but these elderly aircraft have now been withdrawn from front-line service. Afghan attack helicopters (Mi-24 'Hind-D's and Mi-8 'Hip-F's) also carry a three-number code and the national insignia on each side of the tail boom as well as on the underside of the fuselage.

Chinese Shenyang F-4 (MiG-17), F-6 (MiG-19) and F-7 (MiG-21) fighters carry the national markings on wings and fuselage and have an identification number on the nose — three digits in the case of the F-6s (eg 3-34) and four on the F-7s (eg 0208). It is doubtful if any form of regimental insignia is carried although this cannot be confirmed. Transport aircraft, such as the small number of Il-14s in service, display a red and black flag on the rudder together with a small black code derived from the constructor's number identifying the individual machine.

Above: Algeria is one of a number of countries that operate military aircraft with civil registrations. This Lockheed C-130H has 7T WHY on the fin and above the starboard wing.

Angola

As indicated by the insignia, Angola has a Marxist government; the country began receiving aid from the Soviet Union in 1976 following independence from Portugal. In addition to the national markings, the MiG-21s, MiG-23s and Su-22s of the Força Aérea Popular de Angola (Angolan People's Air Force) are given a two-digit number prefixed by the letter C indicating Caça (fighter). Attack helicopters were used extensively by FAPA against UNITA guerrillas in the southeast of the country, the present fleet of Mi-24/25 'Hind's and Mi-8 'Hip's carrying two figures prefixed by the letter H. Second-line types are given a three-letter civilian registration prefixed by the national code D2.

Argentina

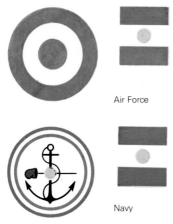

Air Force

Navy

The aircraft roundel has the same colours as the national ensign and on FAA types is carried above and below the wings and on the rear fuselage. The fin flash is an exact miniature of the national flag and includes the 'Sun of May' marking in the centre commemorating the country's independence in 1810. Three-number codes indicate the individual aircraft, each prefixed by a role letter: C for Caza (fighter), B for Bombardeo (bomber), A for Ataque (attack), T for Transporte or H for helicopters. For identification at dispersal, the aircraft number is normally repeated on the nosewheel door. Combat types also carry FUERZA AEREA ARGENTINA in black along the nose.

The blue and white insignia of the Fuerza Aérea Argentina became familiar to British servicemen during the 1982 Falklands War, when Argentina committed her air force to the first major conflict of its existence. The FAA, established as a separate arm in 1945, operated a mixed force of Mirage Vs, Israeli Daggers and A-4 Skyhawks on long-range attack sorties against British targets and gained respect from both sides for the way missions were pressed home against barrages of missiles and gunfire. In the absence of a formal cessation of hostilities, Argentina remained technically at war with Britain.

Unit *esprit de corps* is encouraged by the large badges applied on the fins of the Mirages and Daggers, and on the noses of the Skyhawks. During the Falklands conflict yellow panels were applied to wings, fuselages and tails in an effort to reduce the risk of being fired at by friendly ground forces. These were subsequently removed.

Argentina's naval air arm (Comando de Aviación Naval Argentina) operates Super Etendards and A-4 Skyhawks from both shore bases and the country's sole aircraft carrier, *Veinticinco de Mayo*. An anchor

motif replaces the roundel and is carried above and below the wings, usually in white against dark camouflage and black on light backgrounds. ARMADA is painted on the rear fuselage, while the tail flash is applied across the full width of the rudder and the fin has a blue tip. Naval aircraft carry a prominent unit designator on the fuselage or fin, consisting of the Escuadra (wing) number, a role letter and a three-digit number combining the Escuadrilla (squadron) to which the aircraft is assigned with the number of the individual machine. Thus, Super Etendard 3-A-204, flown by 3ª Escuadra Aeronaval in the Attack role, is operated by 2ª Escuadrilla Aeronaval de Caza y Ataque and is the *fourth* machine in the unit.

Army-operated aircraft and helicopters normally carry a three-digit number prefixed by AE for Aviación del Ejército. An example is AE-413, a Bell UH-1H captured by British forces in the Falklands and now in the UK. Unit badges are painted on the crew entry doors and the word EJERCITO is carried on the tail boom.

Below: The Argentine Navy flew the Dassault Super Etendard carrier-based attack aircraft with dramatic success during the 1982 Falklands war. Note the anchor sign on each wing.

Australia

The present Australian roundel incorporating a kangaroo was adopted after the Second World War and replaced the previous style, which was identical to that used on RAF aircraft. However, the fin flash used on Royal Australian Air Force and Australian Army machines remains similar to the RAF style and is always applied red leading. The roundel is applied to both sides of the forward fuselage of F-111s and F-18 Hornets. 'Miniature' markings are carried on the top of the port wing and on the black-painted underside of the starboard wing of F-111s, the kangaroo always facing forward with its legs toward the wingtip. These swing-wing bombers also carry a small Australian flag at the top of the fin and a unit badge prominently displayed in the form of a yellow flash for 1 Sqn and a blue flash for 6 Sqn. Unit markings of varying kind are also painted on the Hornets as well as on most Australian transport and support aircraft.

The present system of identifying types used by the RAAF, Royal Australian Navy and Australian Army Aviation Corps involves the use of a letter A and a suffix number. The present A-series began in 1961 and followed two previous series, the first of which originated during World War I. The identification number is usually applied on both sides of the rear fuselage between the tailplane and the national insignia, although some aircraft and helicopters carry it on the fin and tailboom respectively.

Army-operated aircraft fall within the RAAF numbering system, but RAN helicopters carry an N prefix followed by the number. The accompanying list of aircraft types and identities (see overleaf) is correct up to February 1992. ▶

RAAF/AAAC aircraft type numbers

A2-	Bell UH-1H Iroquois	US-built, used by RAAF for Army support
A4-	DHC-4 Caribou	RAAF tactical transport
A7-	MB.326H	Standard RAAF jet trainer
A8-	F-111C/RF-111C/F-111A(C)	Main RAAF low-level attack and reconnaissance aircraft
A9-	P-3C Orion	ASW and maritime patrol aircraft
A10-	HS.748	RAAF navigation and VIP aircraft
A11-	Dassault Falcon 20/900	Five VIP aircraft
A14-	PC-6 Turbo-Porter	Army transport and liaison
A15-	CH-47C Chinook	RAAF tactical medium-lift helicopter
A17-	OH-58 Kalkadoon	Australian-built for Army use
A18-	GAF N22M Nomad	Army transport designed and built in Australia
A19-	CT-4A Airtrainer	RAAF basic pilot trainer
A20-	Boeing 707-338C	Four tanker conversions for use with F-18s
A21-	F/A-18 Hornet	Australian-assembled, to replace Mirages
A22-	SA 350 Ecureuil	Trainer and SAR helicopter
A23-	Pilatus PC-9	Advanced Trainer
A25-	S-70A Black Hawk	Tactical Transport
A65-	C-47 Dakota	R & D Trials
A85-	CA-22 Winjeel	FAC
A97-	C-130E/H Hercules	Standard RAAF transport (numbered in previous A-series)

Royal Australian Navy aircraft type numbers

N15-	HS.748	Two ECM aircraft
N16-	Sea King Mk 50/50A	Westland-built, operated on ASW duties
N17-	OH-58 Kalkadoon	Survey support, three operated

Austria

The Osterreichische Luftstreitkräfte (Austrian Air Force) operates 24 Saab J.35Ö Drakens in the air defence role, which is rather more than the number of pilots qualified to fly them. The only other combat type is the Saab 105Ö, which has a light ground attack capability. The former carry air superiority grey while the latter fly in bare metal. National insignia are carried on the forward fuselage and under the port wing and above the starboard wing of the Draken, with a two digit number on the fin. The 105Ö is finished in natural metal, with insignia on the forward fuselage and top and bottom of both wings, while the fin carries' a letter in the Staffel colour, blue, green red or yellow.

Other types in Austrian service are given a number/letter prefix and a two-letter individual code, an example being 3C-JF, an Italian-built AB.206A JetRanger. The current prefix list is: 3C- AB.206A/Bell OH-58B; 3E- Alouette III; 3G- PC-6 Turbo-Porter; 3H-PC-7 Turbo-Trainer; 5D-AB.212; 5S- Short Skyvan.

Bangladesh

Formerly East Pakistan, Bangladesh became an independent state in December 1971 and established a defensive air arm as part of the new country's Defence Forces. The Bang-ladeshi Air Force has never really recovered from the disastrous floods of Spring 1991, which wrote off almost 50 aircraft, many of them F-6s which had only been received from Pakistan during the previous year. Their main interceptor is the Xian F-7M Airguard, of which 16 were supplied by the PRC late in 1989. The F-6s are camouflaged and carry the national insignia on the wings and fuselage, plus a three-digit number of which 628 and 631 are currently flying examples.

Belgium

Air Force

Navy

A member of NATO, Belgium has her military flying units attached to the Alliance's 2nd Allied Tactical Air Force along with British, Dutch and West German elements. The Force Aérienne Belge or Belgische Luchtmacht, depending on whether your language is French or Flemish, groups all flying and non-flying com-bat units — four F-16 and four Mirage 5 escadrilles (squadrons), plus transport and training units — under Tactical Air Command.

The Belgian flag dates back to 1830 when the country gained its independence from the Netherlands, and most FAB combat aircraft carry a representation of this insignia on their fins, black leading on both sides. Roundels, usually thinly outlined in medium blue against a camouflaged background, are applied only on the wings of the F-16s and Mirages, their size having diminished in recent years in accordance with NATO's toned-down markings requirements. Rescue, warning and maintenance stencilling is applied in accordance with NATO standards, the F-16s retaining their factory grey colours together with the markings applied prior to delivery.

The FAB has a number of squadrons with histories going back to World War I and the proud tradi- ▶

F-16 squadron badgess

1 Wing	349 Sqn 'Goedendag' or crossed clubs in a circle
	350 Sqn 'Ambiorix' (Viking head)
10 Wing	23 Sqn Red Devil
	31 Sqn Tiger badge

Mirage 5 squadron badges

2 Wing	2 Sqn red/yellow Comet
3 Wing	1 Sqn Thistle insignia, often in white
	8 Sqn Paper Horse or Cocotte usually in white on a blue background
42 Sqn	Mephisto or winged figure in red within a circle

tions of these units is exemplified by the badges carried on today's aircraft, usually applied to both sides of the aircraft's fin.

All FAB aircraft are assigned a serial number, usually located on the tail and consisting of a two-letter prefix indicating the type of aircraft followed by a sequential number. Current examples are shown in the accompanying table.

The Belgian Army operates Alouette IIs and B-N Islanders and employs the standard national insignia marking. Three Alouette IIIs form a Naval Flight, each machine carrying the roundel with a super-imposed anchor marking in white. A call-sign is also carried (OT-ZPA, -ZPB and -ZPC), this being located on the main cabin door sill in white.

Belgian AF serial numbers

Mirage 5BA	BA 01 to BA 63
Mirage 5BD	BD 01 to BD 16
Mirage 5BR	BR 01 to BR 27
F-16A	FA 01 to FA 94
F-16B	FB 01 to FB 20
Alpha Jet	AT 01 to AT 33
C-130H Hercules	CH 01 to CH 12
HS.748	CS 01 to CS 03
SA-26T Merlin IIA	CF 01 to CF 06
SF.260MB	ST 01 to ST 36
CM.170R Magister	MT 01 to MT 50
Sea King Mk 48	RS 01 to RS 05

Benin

Formerly called Dahomey, the small former French colony of Benin currently has no combat aircraft within the Forces Armées Populaires du Benin, operating instead a modest collection of transport and liaison types. Aircraft in use include some Douglas C-47s, Antonov An-26s and two DO.128s. As well as the national insignia, aircraft carry registrations such as TY-ACC, which is applied to a C-47.

Bolivia

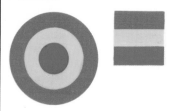

A handful of ex-Venezuelan F-86F Sabres have formed the fighter backbone of the Fuerza Aérea

Brazil

The largest and best equipped air arm in South America, the Forca Aerea buys much of its hardware from indigenous sources. The cutting edge currently consists of 20 Mirage IIIs and 55 F-5E/B/Fs, while in the attack role, the Italo-Brazilian AMX is beginning to enter large scale service, with 79 single seaters and 15 two seater AMX(T)s on order. They are supplemented in the light attack/COIN role by 104 EMB-326 Xavantes.

The national star insignia is formed from the colours on the Brazilian flag and is carried on the wings and fuselage of most FAB aircraft. The exceptions are the Mirages and F-5Es which have the marking only on the wings in miniature form against, respectively, blue-grey and three-tone Vietnam-style camouflage. On tactical aircraft a small yellow-green flash is carried on the fin, while non-camouflaged support and training types have these colours painted on the rudders, usually to the full width and depth. Unit or Grupo badges are also carried, usually on the fin or nose, and transport aircraft bear FORCA AEREA BRASILEIRA on the fuselage.

Boliviana for a number of years, as attempts to replace them with more modern equipment have been thwarted by financial problems. Just four Sabres, in dark grey, green and mid grey camouflage, remain in the inventory, backed by thirty plus T-33s resplendent in green, brown and tan. Undersides of both types are finbished in pale grey. FAB aircraft carry the roundel marking on the wings and fuselage, together with the national colours applied across the rudder in equal segments with red at the top. Black numbers (eg, 651, 652, 656) are painted on the fin of the Sabres, while the T-33s have a small three-figure number in black on the nose and fin, prefixed by FAB. Support and training aircraft such as the PC-7s have large numbers on the fuselage prefixed FAB. Badges and flamboyant nose markings (shark mouths and eagle's heads) feature on many FAB aircraft, but particularly the PC-7s, of which 22 remain. Transport aircraft carry registrations in the series TAM-01.

Above: This Brazilian F-5F wears the South East Asia camouflage scheme, with the national star under each wing.

Serialling is in four-digit number blocks, the first number indicating the basic role:
0 and 1 — training; 2 — transport; 3 — liaison; 4 — fighter; 5 — bomber; 6 — amphibian; 7 — maritime patrol; 8 — helicopters.
The other three digits represent the individual aircraft and the last two are repeated larger on the nose. Every Brazilian military aircraft is given a type designation and this also appears on the fin as a prefix to the number. Current examples are as shown.

The Brazilian Navy is a helicopter operator (fixed-wing types such as the carrier-borne Trackers coming under FAB control) and employs a green-yellow-blue roundel as its standard insignia. Serials are prefixed N and are carried on the tail booms of the Sea Kings, Lynx and Ecureuils, while MARINHA in bold letters identifies naval machines.

Brazilian type designations

A-1	AMX
H-1	UH-1 Iroquois
OH/VH-4	Bell 206 Jetranger
F-5B/E	F-5B/E
U-7	EMB-810 Seneca II
EC-9	EMB-121 Xingu
H-13	OH-13 Sioux
P-16E	S-2E Tracker
UP-16A	US-2A Tracker
U-19	EMB-201 Ipanema
T-23	A122 Uirapuru
T-25	N621 Universal
AT-26	EMB-326 Xavante
T-27	EMB-312 Tucano
CH-33	SA.330 Puma
CH-34	AS.332 Super Puma
C-42/L-42	N591 Regente
CH-50	SA.350 Ecureuil I
CH/VH-55	SA.355 Ecureuil II
C-91	BAe Hs 748
VU/VC-93	BAe Hs 125
C/EC/P/R-95	EMB-110 Bandeirante
VC-96	Boeing 737
VC-97	ERMB-120 Brasilia
F-103	Mirage III
C-115	DHC-5 Buffalo
C-130	C-130 Hercules
KC-137	Boeing KC-707

Bulgaria

The Bulgarian national insignia, currently a red star enclosing a roundel in green, red and white, the national colours; is since the dissolution of the Warsaw Pact, in the process of being amended to become a roundel only. In this form it will be located on the wings and fuselages of Bulgarian Air Force combat aircraft (MiG-17, 21, 23, 25, and 29, and Su-22 and 25) and on the fins of transport types (An-24).

Below: One of the few photographs of Bulgarian military aircraft, this picture shows the tail markings and red identification numbers on MiG-21MF fighters.

Burma (Myanmar)

Tamdaw Lay, the Myanmar Air Arm, is in the early 1990s upgrading its capabilities, perhaps with a view to countering guerrilla activity along the Laotian border. The mixed fleet of AT-33s and SF. 260Ws have been withdrawn from service, as were 10 Bell 47G helicopters. By July 1991, 20 Super Galebs had been delivered, while an order for 38 F-7M Airguard and F-6 fighters was placed with the PRC during 1990. In addition, 12 W-3 Sokol helicopters were acquired from Poland during that year. The triangular insignia, which bears no relationship to the Myanmar flag, is carried on fuselage and wings. Aircraft have a serial number which serves as both unit and individual identification. These have in the past sometimes been prefixed by UB for Union of Burma, and are often applied in Myanmarian script.

Recent examples are: PC-7s 2301-2316; Bell UH-1Hs 6201-6218; and Alouette IIIs 6101-6114. The numbers are sometimes split on the fuselage by the national insignia and applied in white on a camouflaged background, or painted close together on the aft fuselage.

Cameroun

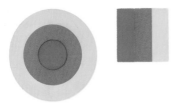

This former French colony gained independence in 1960 and established a small air arm, 'Armée de l'Air du Cameroun' operating some transport and liaison aircraft. A counter-insurgency and light attack element was then added, which currently consists of five AlphaJets and ten CM-170 Magisters, efforts to acquire Kfirs and Mirage F.1s having foundered. The national marking is formed from the pan-African colours and when used as rudder striping, with green leading, a yellow star of liberty is applied centrally on the red segment. Aircraft carry a registration in the TJ- XAA to -XZZ block, examples being Lockheed C-130H TJ-XAC, Alphajet TJ-XBV and DHC-5 Buffalo TJ- XBT. Unit badges are worn on the noses of the Hercules, with CAMEROUN AIR FORCES applied on the forward fuselage.

Canada

Standard

Low-visibility

As a member of NATO, Canada has maintained a presence in Germany for many years, the air element of which is known as the 1st Canadian Air Division, with two squadrons of CF-18 Hornets (Nos 421 and 439) at Baden-Sollingen and some CH-136 Kiowa helicopters at Lahr. The Hornets will be returned to Canada by 1994 and reassigned to air defence duties. The remainder of the 125 Hornets, the last of which was delivered in 1988, are homebased. 18 CP-140 Aurora maritime patrol and three CP-140A Arcturus surveillance aircraft are on strength, with a numerically large force of transports, trainers and helicopters.

The maple leaf insignia was adopted by the Royal Canadian Air Force after the end of World War I. In slightly modified form it continues to be the national marking of what has since 1988 been the Canadian Armed Forces — Air and is carried in low visibility form on the wings and fuselage of the present equipment. Under Canadian law, titling in English has to be repeated in French and *vice versa*, hence ARMED FORCES — FORCES ARMEES applied either side of the fuselage roundel on CAF aircraft. On the Hornets, the word CANADA is carried mid-way along the fuselage, while on the outside of the fins is the national flag insignia in dark grey together with the serial number. Unit badges are painted unobtrusively on the fin tips, again in dark grey against the light grey camouflage background. Canada is the only country to have officially adopted a scheme experimented with by a number of western air forces, the painting of a false cockpit on the underside of the nose of its Hornets. This takes the form of a dark grey outline aligned with the pilot's canopy. The individual aircraft number is applied under the port wing, and CAF under the starboard, mid-way between tip and root.

Canadian military aircraft are given a type designation comprising a role prefix, preceded in all cases by the letter C, and followed by a sequential number. Current examples are as listed on the following page. ▶

Canadian type designations

CC-109	CL-66B Cosmopolitan
CH-113/A	Labrador/Voyageur
CT-114	Canadair CL-41 Tutor
CC-115	DHC-5 Buffalo
CH-118	Bell UH-1H Iroquois
CH-124A/U	Sikorsky SH-3A
CC-130E/H	Lockheed Hercules
CT-133	T-33AN Silver Star
CT-134/A	Beech Musketeer
CH-135	Bell CUH-1N
CH-136	Bell OH-58A Kiowa
CC-137	Boeing 707
CC-138	DHC-6 Twin Otter
CH-139	Bell 206 JetRanger III
CP-140/A	Aurora/Arcturus
CC/CT-142	DHC-8M Dash 8
CH-143	MBB BK.117
CT-144	Canadair Challenger
CT-145	Beech Super King Air
CH-147	Boeing CH-47C
CF-188A/B	F/A-18A/B Hornet

Serial numbers normally carried on the aircraft tail incorporate the designation but omit the letter prefix and are followed by a sequential number of up to three digits. Thus 188745 signifies a CF-18 assigned the serial number 745, which is often repeated on the aircraft nose as well as under the port wing.

Chad

The Force Aerienne Tchadienne was formed with French assistance in 1973 and operated six Douglas Skyraiders for some years before a civil war, attrition and the general vulnerability of these old piston-engined bombers forced their withdrawal. The combat aircraft element currently consists of two armed Pilatus PC-7s, and three SF-260Ws captured during the recent conflict with Libya. Transports constitute the main type of equipment; among those in current service are three C-47s, two DC-4s, four C-130s, two C-212 Aviocars, and a single Caravelle VIR for VIP duties. Two PC-6B Turbo Porters, five Cessna FTB.337s and two remaining Broussards are used for communications duties.

Chile

Air Force

Navy

Low-visibility

Chilean military aircraft carry the main components of the national flag in the form of a white star on a shield

Above: Canada plans to have 138 CF-18s. These two-seaters of 410 Sqn are in standard toned-down colours (FS 35237 blue-grey on upper surface, FS 36118 dark grey for false canopy).

Central African Republic

Originally part of French Equatorial Africa, this relatively poor country allocates only a minimal sum to defence and its air arm. The latter's main tasks are civil assistance flights using C-47s and Macchi AL60 transports. Military aircraft operated by the Force Aérienne Centrafricaine are allocated designations from TL-KAA. Civil types also carry the TL prefix. No combat aircraft are on strength at present, an order for 12 Pucaras having been cancelled.

in blue and red, representing the snow on the Andes mountains, the sky above and the blood shed by the nation's patriots. In this form it is usually located only above the starboard wing and under the port wing, the opposite positions being occupied by the individual aircraft

Above: Chilean Air Force A-37B light attack aircraft showing the positioning of the wing insignia and individual aircraft number.

number. The white star appears on the rudder of all aircraft, either over the camouflage or on a specially ▶

27

painted dark blue background. There are exceptions to every rule, and the two Boeing 707s operated by the Fuerza Aerea de Chile have a large white star applied in the centre of the all-blue fin and rudder. They also have the air force title painted along the fuselage.

Fuerza Aerea de Chile aircraft are allocated serials in blocks; jet-powered aircraft have J prefixes to three-digit numbers.

Helicopters have serials beginning with H, while other types wear unprefixed numbers in the following ranges: trainers 100 and 400, light transports 200, medium transports 300 and miscellaneous aircraft and

FAeCh jet aircraft serials

J-500-515	Dassault Mirage 50 interceptors
J-600-	Cessna A-37B close-support aircraft
J-700-	Hawker Hunter fighters
J-800-817	Northrop F-5E/F fighters
J-370-	Cessna T-37B/C trainers

Colombia

The multi-coloured national insignia, applied to Colombian military aircraft for more than 40 years, bears little resemblance to the country's flag. The horizontal rudder striping is a closer representation, this being carried on all aircraft operated by the Fuerza Aerea Colombiana, the red and yellow colours symbolising the nation's Spanish origins.

The roundel is carried on the fuselage and wings of most types, including the 13 Kfir C.7/TC.7s delivered in 1989, 14 Mirage 5COA fighters, COR reconnaissance and two seater COD trainers; the surviving T-33s having been grounded. Cessna A-37Bs operate in the attack role, painted in dark disruptive camouflage of dark green, tan and black. All aircraft carry FAC on their fins above the serial number, the latter being repeated under the port wing and above the starboard wing. The roundel ocupies the opposite position on the wings.

Serials are allocated in three- and four-digit blocks, examples being FAC 902 on a Douglas DC-6 and 3023 on a Mirage 5COA fighter. A suffix letter applied to a serial indicates a replacement aircraft for one lost (eg, 306A on a T-34). Numbers in the 1100

heavy transports 900. The serial number features prominently on the rear fuselage or tail of most types. One anomaly with the above system is the apparent numbering of the three ex-RAF Canberra PR.9s, delivered to the FAeCh in 1982, as 341, 342 and 343. As these are hardly medium transports, the whole system would appear subject to variation.

Chilean naval aircraft, including six EMB-111ANS for maritime patrol plus Bandeirante transports and Lynx ASW helicopters, carry the insignia with anchor motif.

---

to 1199 block are reserved for aircraft operated by the military airline, Satena, which flies a number of types on internal routes within Colombia. FUERZA AEREA COLOMBIANA is normally applied to the fuselages of transport aircraft and the rear booms of helicopters, while the majority of stencilling is in Spanish such as HELICE for propeller and RESCATE for rescue.

Below: This Mirage 5COA in Colombian service is painted in a green/grey camouflage scheme. The national insignia is applied to the front fuselage and upper wing, with horizontal stripes on the rudder. The fuselage marking is marred by the auxiliary intake door.

China

The Air Force of the People's Liberation Army is the third largest air arm in the world with an estimated strength of some 4,750 aircraft. It is organized along Soviet lines with up to four squadrons, each with about 15 aircraft, forming an Air Regiment, and three Regiments making up an Air Division. The Xian J-6 Farmer is the numerically most important fighter type, although badly dated. About 250 F-7 Fishbeds are in service, and at Le Bourget 1991 an artist's impression was released of a solid nosed version, the Super Seven, due to fly in 1993. About 100 twin engined J-8s Finbacks are in service, but the much improved J-8II appears to have foundered. Late in 1991 the new J-9 was announced, but virtually nothing is known of this, while 22 Su-Flankers were acquired from Russia during 1991-92.

The Chinese national star and bar marking is carried on all these aircraft and on the H-5 (Il-28) and H-6 (Tu-16) bombers, located prominently on each side of the rear fuselage and on the wings. The central motif of the star contains the Chinese characters 8 over 1. Code numbers on the noses and on engine nacelles of military aircraft are formed of five digits, often in stencil-split style, and painted in a number of colours including red, black and yellow. Most fighter and attack aircraft appear to be unpainted, although some examples of the Qiang-5 carry a green disruptive camouflage over the top surfaces. Also observed on the Qiang-5 is an unusual marking combination painted on the outside of the large wing fence and on the fuselage. This is believed to be intended for formation flying: viewed from the rear three-quarter position, the two designs merge to form one pattern.

Congo

The Force Aerienne Congolaise has a small combat element consisting of at most 14 MiG-21 Fishbeds and eight MiG-17 Frescos, with a single MiG-15UTI Midget conversion trainer. A small transport fleet consists of seven An-24 Cokes, one An-26 Curl, three Noratlas, two C-47s and an Il-14 Crate. Two Mi-8 Hip and four Alouette helicopters round out the force. The roundel is applied to the wings and fuselage, while a fin flash is a replica of the national flag. Aircraft serials are prefixed TN and have three digits.

Cuba

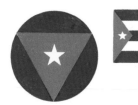

Operating equipment almost entirely supplied by the Soviet Union, the Fuerza Aérea Revolucionaria indulges in hardly any spectacular colouring on its combat aircraft. The roundel marking is carried on the wings and fuselage of most aircraft and the rudder striping is a repeat of the national flag but incorporating an isosceles triangle with a small star on the trailing edge.

Latest estimates show a total of about 550 aircraft in service with the FAR. MiG-29 Fulcrums entered service in 1990, although whether the 36 ordered will all be delivered remains to be seen. MiG-23S/BN Floggers are otherwise the most up to date fighters in the inventory, supplemented by 185 MiG-21 Fishbeds and a handful of MiG-19 Farmers and MiG-17 Frescos. Fulcrum wears a blue/grey air superiority finish, while Flogger has typical Russian green/ brown camouflage.

Anti-tank and close air support duties are carried out by a fleet of around 15 Mi-25 Hind D assault helicopters.

FAR serialling appears somewhat haphazard. Numbers carried on the MiG-21s range between 103 and 663 and the MiG-17s are in the 200-range, while one MiG-23 is 710. Tactical transports such as the fleet of 20 An-26s have four-digit serials.

Czechoslovakia

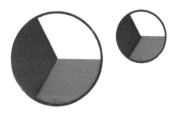

With the dissolution of the Warsaw Pact on 1 April 1991, the way became clear for the Ceskoslovenske Letectvo to adopt an RAF style organisation of squadrons, wings, and groups. Numerically, the most important type in service is the MiG-21, with more than 300 operated in the fighter, reconnaissance and training roles. 12 MiG-29s have also been delivered. MiG-23s in both fighter and ground-attack versions total about 80, supported by over 80 Su-22 Fitter K attack and reconnaissance aircraft. From 1985, the Su-25 Frogfoot close support aircraft joined the inventory, and 38 are currently backed by 45 Mil-24 Hind D assault helicopters.

Since they are used in tactical roles, almost all front-line Czech Air

Force aircraft are camouflaged in green and brown disruptive schemes with light blue underneath. Over this is applied the national marking, formed from the colours of the former Austrian provinces of Bohemia (red and white) and Moravia (blue). It is located above and below each wing and on both sides of the fin with blue foremost. Serials are usually applied on the forward fuselage in black, although MiG-23s have been seen carrying the four-digit number on the intakes in black outlined in white. Mi-24s also have four-figure numbers, but carried on the rear tail booms.

Personal or unit markings are almost unheard of in the East European air forces, but in the mid-1970s one MiG-21 was seen with a black and white chequered rudder and a small emblem on the nose showing a wolf's head on a green shield. This attempt at introducing some sort of individualism into the Service appears not to have been repeated.

Below: A Czech MiG-23MF 'Flogger-B' in disruptive green/brown camouflage. Its black four-digit identification number, outlined in white, is on the side of the engine intake.

Denmark

This NATO country operates a combat force of more than 40 Saab 35 Drakens and 50 General Dynamics F-16s. The Drakens are assigned to the attack role and are camouflaged in non-reflective dark olive drab and light grey, with low-visibility roundels and fin flashes. The F-16s are tasked with air defence and carry the standard factory finish of three greys together with miniature markings. The red and white markings have

been used on Danish military aircraft since the First World War and the fin flash is a representation of the national flag or *Dannebrog*.

Every Royal Danish Air Force (Kongelige Danske Flyvevåbnet) aircraft carries an individual letter/number code comprising one or two prefix letters followed by a three-digit number. This number is formed from the last three digits of the aircraft's construction number. An example is Draken A-008 which was built by Saab and given the c/n 351008. The codes and serials of the present RDAF combat force are as shown (see overleaf).

RDAF transport and training aircraft often carry the Service badge on the forward fuselage, while Lynx helicopters operated by the Danish ▶

Royal Danish Air Force aircraft codes

Saab F35 Draken	A-001 to A-020	Attack aircraft
Saab RF35 Draken	AR-101 to AR-120	Reconnaissance aircraft
Saab TF35 Draken	AT-151 to AT-161	Combat trainers
General Dynamics F-16A	E-174 to E-611	Interceptors
General Dynamics F-16B	ET-204 to ET-615	Combat trainers

Naval Air Service carry an anchor insignia on the cabin. The latter are operated from frigates of the Danish Navy and carry the serials S-134, -142, -170, -175, -181, -187, -191 and -196.

Below: ET-205 is a Danish F-16B, seen here painted in the two-tone grey 'Compass Ghost' scheme. The radomes on Danish and other F-16s are currently also painted grey.

Dominica

Eight Cessna A-37B Dragonflies constitute the only jet-powered combat element of the Fuerza Aérea Dominicana, although the service-ability of these ageing aircraft must be marginal. The Dominican roundel is based on the national flag and is carried on the fuselage as well as on the top surface of the port wing and the lower surface of the starboard wing. The letters FAD are applied to the fin above the aircraft serial number. Other fixed-wing assets include a squadron of O-2A Skymasters in the liaison/COIN/FAC roles. A grey camouflage finish has been applied to the aircraft.

Ecuador

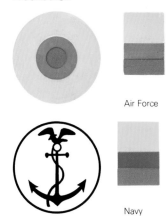

Air Force

Navy

Rather confusingly, Ecuador has a national flag almost identical to that of neighbouring Colombia, the only differences being in the shade of blue and the proportions of the flag. On aircraft flown by the Ecuadorian Air Force (Fuerza Aérea Ecuatoriana) both the roundel and the rudder or fin flash have the colours in proportions directly related to those of the flag.

Ecuador has one of the best equipped air arms in the area and is able to field Mirage F.1s, Jaguar fighter-bombers, Kfir interceptors and Strikemaster and A-37B Dragonfly attack aircraft. Most of these types are camouflaged, some in the air force's own adopted style of brown and tan, and others in green/grey (Jaguars) or green/brown (Mirage F.1s). The roundel is normally applied above the port wing and below the starboard wing, the opposite positions being occupied by the letters FAE in black and, in some cases, the aircraft serial number. FAE aircraft generally use the construction number or the last three digits of it as their identification serial.

Transport aircraft carry FUERZA AEREA ECUATORIANA somewhere on the fuselage and include the civil registration on the fin alongside the military serial number. Ecuadorian registrations are prefixed HC. Some FAE aircraft carry prefixes to the serial such as BE for the currently withdrawn Canberras, and TP for the Cessna T-41D trainers. Badges are sometimes worn, usually on the nose, to denote the operating unit.

Air elements of the Ecuadorian Army carry the name EJERCITO, while Navy-operated aircraft have NAVAL in prominent letters on the fuselage, an anchor motif on the fin and serials prefixed ANE. Both these Services carry roundels on the wings together with the relevant serials, in the same style as FAE machines.

Below: Ecuador's Jaguars were all delivered in standard RAF green/grey camouflage. Only the fin marking identifies the user.

Egypt

Once almost entirely comprised of Eastern Bloc aircraft, the Arab Republic of Egypt Air Force has largely re-equipped with Western machines, the latest contract signed in April 1991 for 46 F-16C/Ds bringing the total of this type to 165, including 38 earlier F-16A/Bs. In addition, a squadron of 18 Dassault Mirage 2000E/Bs have been operated as interceptors since October 1987, while four Grumman E-2C Hawkeyes, with a further one on order, fill the AEW role.

The remainder of the combat fleet is rather a mixed bag. Eighty Mirage 5s and 32 F-4E Phantoms are supplemented by 97 MiG-21MF and 52 Chinese-built F-7 Fishbeds, 92 obsolete F-6 Farmers, and 32 even more dated MiG-17 Frescos. Nine Tupolev Tu-16K Badgers are retained for the anti-shipping role, while 45 AlphaJet MS1/MS2s, built in Egypt under licence, double for advanced training and light attack.

The in-flight refuelling role will soon be carried out by three con-

Below: Under Peace Vector, Egypt received 9301, the first of 80 F-16s, in early 1982. The aircraft carry basic insignia and standard Middle Grey/ Underbelly Grey colours.

verted Boeing 707s, while the backbone of the fixed-wing transport fleet comprises about 25 C-130H Hercules. Rotary wing machines include some 90 SA.342L Gazelles in the attack role, and transport duties are undertaken by 14 Italian-built CH-47C Chinooks, over 25 Westland Commandos, at least 59 Mi-8 Hips and around half a dozen Mi-6 Hooks.

All these aircraft carry the EAF roundel on wings and fuselage, while on the fin is a small reproduction of the national flag. Serials are formed of four numbers applied in Arabic style on the nose or, in the case of the Mirages, on the rear fuselage.

Unit badges are rare, although small designs have been noted on some MiG-21s. The F-16s, Mirage 2000s and Phantoms all wear air superiority finishes while the remainder, with a few natural metal exceptions, carry desert camouflage. An interesting variation seen on an upgraded MiG-21 in 1990 was decked out in chocolate brown, pale green an an almost lemon yellow! Many EAF combat aircraft, including F-16s, carry large areas of orange bordered in black on wings, fins and dorsal spines, apparently a visual identification measure in close combat.

Below: F-4E Phantom, USAF serial 66-0366, has Egyptian serial 7813 in Arabic script on the nose. The sale of Egypt's Phantoms to Turkey had been rumoured for some time.

0	1	2	3	4
٠	١	٢	٣	٤
5	6	7	8	9
٥	٦	٧	٨	٩

Ethiopia

The Ethiopian Air Force roundel is formed from the colours of the national flag and is applied in the standard positions on each EAF aircraft. The serial numbers applied on the fins do not appear to follow any logical sequence, three de Havilland Doves obtained many years ago being numbered 801-803 and four

Canberra B.52 bombers bought in the late 1960s carrying 351-354. These machines, like all other Western aircraft, have been retired for some considerable time due to an almost total lack of spares. The front line force currently consists of about 50 MiG-23 Floggers and 60 MiG-21 Fishbeds, with 30 plus Mi-24 Hinds and 35 Mil-8 Hips in the assault helicopter role. Israel has agreed to supply a squadron of 15 Kfirs, but this has been blocked by the USA, and it seems unlikely that they will now be delivered. The transport fleet consists mainly of An-12 Cubs, of which at least eleven are reported to be still in service.

Finland

The present Finnish Air Force (Ilmavoimat) roundel replaced the original blue swastika on a white field towards the end of World War II. It now adorns all Finnish military aircraft and helicopters. Under the terms of the 1947 Treaty of Paris, the Finnish AF is officially limited to a strength of 60 combat aircraft. The three air defence wings which currently make up the air arm are equipped with 45 Saab J35 Drakens and 29 MiG-21s. Both are due for replacement; JAS-39 Gripen, F-16 and Mirage 2000-S are all under consideration. Over 50 Hawks are in service in the training role, taking student pilots from initial training before passing them on to the squadrons for type conversion.

The Finnish system of identifying aircraft consists of a two-letter prefix denoting the aircraft type, followed by a sequential number of up to three digits. This marking is carried on the rear fuselage or helicopter tail boom. Both the Drakens and the MiG-21s carry a disruptive camouflage scheme over the top surfaces of dark green and dark grey with light grey on the undersides.

Finnish Air Force identification serials

Saab J35 Draken	DK-201 to 271 (27 in service by late-1985)
MiG-21bis/UM	MG-111 to 144 (29 'bis' and two UM)
BAe Hawk T.51	HW-301 to 350
Fokker F.27-100 Friendship	FF-1 to FF-3
Potez CM.170 Magister	FM-1 to 82 (small number remain in use)
VL Vinka	VN-1 to 30

France

Air Force

Navy

It is to France that credit should be given for establishing a basic form of military aircraft marking: on July 26, 1912, an official French Army order decreed that roundels should be applied to the wings and fuselage of all military flying machines. The concentric rings of red, white and blue laid down then have survived to the present day. From 1945, a narrow yellow outline was added to ensure that the marking stood out against camouflage paint or the natural metal finish retained by many aircraft in the post-war years, but in 1982 French military aircraft, like those of other Western air forces, underwent a toning-down process whereby the roundel diminished in size — from 80cm to 58cm in the case of the Mirage III, for example — and lost its yellow surround.

Rudder stripes, which also originated before World War I, began to disappear from French combat aircraft in the early 1970s, although examples can still be seen applied to second-line types. The stripes are carried in the order blue/white/red from front to rear on both sides of the tail. The aircraft manufacturer, mark

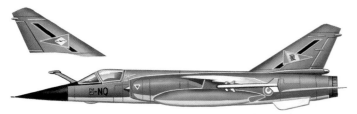

Above: 5 Escadre de Chasse at Orange was the second Wing to equip with the Mirage F.1. This

F.1C-200 has the two escadrille badges on the fin, SPA124 (Joan of Arc) port and SPA26 (stork).

Above: A Jaguar of the fourth squadron of Escadre de Chasse 11, operating from Toul and

Bordeaux. The fin carries the two escadrille badges and on the intake is the Wing number.

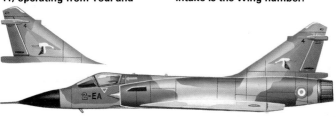

Above: It was predictable that EC2 at Dijon, the famous Cigognes Wing, would be the

first unit to receive the Mirage 2000 interceptor. Note the rear location of the fuselage roundel.

number and construction number may be stencilled in black on the rudder and often over the stripes.

Coloured badges are also painted on the fin. Usually a different one is carried on each side, reflecting current Armée de l'Air unit organisation. An Escadre, composed of up to four Escadrons, is the basic unit; each Escadron is formed by two Escadrilles, and it is the badges of both these elements which are normally displayed on either side. For example, the 12 Escadre de Chasse is made up of EC1/12, EC2/12 and EC3/12: Mirage F1.Cs of EC1/12 would carry the codes 12-YA to 12-YZ on their noses, the number indicating the Escadre, Y the first Escadron and the final letter being

the individual aircraft in the escadron. The number is often applied stencil-split in black outline followed by the letters in stencil-split solid black. In this case the left-hand side of the nose would carry a hornet of SPA89 while the right-hand has a tiger's head of SPA162, the first and second Escadrilles respectively.

Rescue and maintenance information around the airframe takes the form of standard NATO markings and these too have undergone changes to reduce their visibility. Ejection seat markings are now generally applied in red and black with the white deleted, while the prominent red/yellow wing-walk markings on the wings of Mirages have had the yellow deleted. ▶

Above: One of the three squadrons forming EC5 at Orange operates as a conversion unit for all French Air Force Mirage F.1 Wings. This two-seat F.1B combat trainer carries a large Super 530 air-to-air missile underwing and a dummy Magic round on the wingtip. Behind the Wing number and individual aircraft letters are the two ejection seat triangles, while behind the rear cockpit are the ground rescue instructions.

Left: French Army Gazelle and Puma helicopters have recently adopted the legend 'armee de TERRE' on their rear tailbooms. As this example of the former type shows, the roundel is retained. Leaving the launch tube of this SA. 342M is a HOT wire-guided anti-tank missile.

Aéronavale

The French Naval Air Arm has a front-line force of Super Etendards, Etendards, F-8E(FN) Crusaders, Atlantics, Alizés, Super Frelons and Lynx helicopters. Units operating these types are numbered and carry a suffix letter F for *Flotille*. Second-line units carry the suffix S for *Escadrille de Servitude*. Examples are 14F, which flies Super Etendards from Landivisiau, and 11S, equipped with Xingu transports at Dugny.

Naval aircraft carry roundels on the wings and fuselage with a black anchor superimposed. In 1984, a two-tone grey colour scheme was tested on Super Etendards and Etendards, with the result that the roundel lost its yellow outline and the individual aircraft number was changed from white to grey. Note that Aéronavale aircraft carry the wing roundel only on the upper left ▶

and lower right surfaces; in the other positions is the aircraft number. This is principally for ease of identification during carrier operations.

The legend MARINE can be applied on the aft fuselage in black (eg Crusaders) or white (eg Lynx and Super Frelon). Unit badges tend to be less flamboyant in application on naval aircraft than those on AdlA machines; when carried, their usual positions are under the cockpit (Crusader) and at the base of the leading edge of the fin (Super Etendard).

Aviation Légère de l'Armée de Terre

French Army Aviation is mainly composed of Gazelle and Alouette II/III light helicopters plus Puma trans-

Above: The Aeronavale uses a disruptive blue-grey camouflage for its Super Etendards.

Right: Mirage 2000 interceptors wear the roundel at the rear of the fuselage.

port/troop carriers. The machines are allocated to military units at divisional level and only a few markings are carried. The most prominent of these is the three-letter code indicating the individual peloton or escadrille, usually carried each side of the main cabin, and ARMEE DE TERRE applied along the tail booms of most of the Gazelles and Pumas currently in use. A small roundel is usually carried towards the rear of the main cabin.

French callsign blocks in current use

F-BAAA to -BZZZ	Civil flying registrations. Series used since 1940
F-CAAA to -CZZZ	Current gliders
F-MAAA to -MZZZ	Army Aviation (Aviation Légère de l'Armée de Terre)
F-MJAA to -MJZZ	Gendarmerie or Police-operated aircraft and helicopters
F-MMAA to -MMZZ	Army Aviation (ALAT)
F-OAAA to -OZZZ	French overseas civil aircraft
F-PAAA to -PZZZ	Provisional civil registrations
F-RAAA to -ULZZ	Armée de l'Air
F-VAAA to -VAZZ	Civil delivery flights
F-WAAA to -WZZZ	Experimental and prototype aircraft/helicopters
F-XAAA to -YZZZ	Aéronavale
F-ZAAA to -ZAZZ	Aircraft/helicopters under evaluation
F-ZBAA to -ZBBZ	Protection Civile
F-ZBCA to -ZWZZ	State organizations, trials and support aircraft

Gabon

Nine Dassault Mirage 5 fighter-bombers acquired by the Forces Aériennes Gabonaises constitute the country's front-line combat strength. While some were ordered as new-build aircraft, later machines were supplied from ex- Libyan stocks and include some two- seat Mirage 5DG

trainers. These aircraft carry a disruptive camouflage scheme of green and grey over their top surfaces with the Gabon roundel on the intake sides and the wings. Three-digit identification serials are carried. Hercules transport aircraft of the FAG have the full name of the air force applied on the forward fuselage and a civilian registration painted on the fin, TR-KKB and TR-KKC being two examples. Prominently displayed at the top of the fin is a reproduction of the national flag. VIP aircraft have the legend REPUBLIQUE GABONAISE on the sides of the fuselage.

Germany

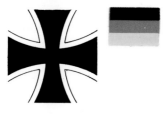

The familiar iron cross of the German Air Force, or Luftwaffe, bears a close similarity to that displayed on aircraft dating back to World War I and was adopted in the mid-1950s when the re-formed air arm was constituted. A miniature national flag was also chosen for the fin flash. Since 1968 Luftwaffe aircraft have been identified by four-digit serial numbers, usually split by the national marking. The current range is divided into serial blocks allocated to aircraft roles.

Luftwaffe serial blocks

0001-0999	Experimental aircraft
1001-1999	VIP and staff transports
2001-4999	Front-line combat aircraft
5001-5999	Transport aircraft
6001-6999	Maritime patrol aircraft
7001-7999	Light helicopters
8001-8999	Medium helicopters
9001-9999	Trainers

Under this system, in which the numbers are usually sequential, McDonnell Douglas RF-4E Phantom 35 + 03 is the third machine of the type obtained by the service. A total of 88 of these reconnaissance Phantoms were bought.

The Luftwaffe currently operates five main types of combat aircraft: Panavia Tornado (all-weather strike), F-4F and RF-4E Phantom (fighter-bomber and reconnaissance), Mikoyan MiG-29 Fulcrum (air superiority) and Dassault-Breguet/Dornier AlphaJet (light attack/ close-support). The Fulcrums, of which there are twenty, have been inherited from the now defunct East German Luftstreitkrafte. Interceptor F-4Fs are being upgraded with the Hughes APG-65 radar, and given an Amraam capability, a programme which

Above: Panavia Tornado 44 + 43 of JaboG 32 wears the dark grey/dark green/medium green colour scheme now standard on Luftwaffe Tornados. Note the fuel tank and pylon are still in the earlier mid-grey finish. The unit shield is shown on the fin and the national markings are on the port upper and starboard lower wings.

should be completed during 1992. Replacement by EFA was scheduled to commence in 1997, although recent political decisions make this unlikely. The codes and badges applied to each of these major warplanes and the units operating them are detailed on page 44.

The camouflage schemes used on Luftwaffe aircraft are detailed in the chapter on the subject. Note that all German military aircraft carry standard NATO maintenance, rescue and servicing markings (see the United Kingdom entry for examples), some in toned-down form to reduce brightness on the later types of camouflage.

Bundesmarine

The German naval air arm combines Tornado fixed-wing combat aircraft

with ASW aircraft (Atlantics) and SAR/ASV helicopters (Lynx and Sea Kings). The service has a distinctive camouflage scheme of basalt grey (RAL7012) and pale grey (RAL7035) and its aircraft wear the black anchor symbol together with the legend MARINE.

Marinefliegergeschwader 1, or MFG 1, is based at Schleswig and flies ▶

Above: The badge identifies this F-4F Phantom as being from JaboG 36 at Hopsten. Partly hidden by the intake splitter plate are the dual language (German and English) rescue instructions which are applied to all aircraft operated by NATO. The beige marking at lower right is a low-light formation strip.

Luftwaffe combat units, aircraft serials and badges

Panavia Tornado: 43 + 01 to 46 + 57 to date

JaboG 31 'Boelcke'	Winged sword on shield
JaboG 32	Bird with bomb insignia
JaboG 33	Stylized bird on lozenge-shaped shield
JaboG 34	Two paper darts over mountains on shield

McDonnell Douglas F-4F Phantom: 37 + 01 to 38 + 75

JaboG 35	Eagle's head emblem
JaboG 36	Prancing horse in shield
JG 71 'Richthofen'	Red R on white shield
JG 74 'Molders'	Paper dart on circular shield

McDonnell Douglas RF-4E Phantom: 35 + 01 to 35 + 88

AG 51 'Immelmann'	Owl emblem
AG 52	Panther head

AlphaJet: 40 + 01 to 41 + 75

JaboG 41	Eagle's head in outline
JaboG 43	Two darts and Viking ship prow
JaboG 44	Lion and NATO symbol
JaboG 49	Diving eagle and lightning flash

JaboG 35 is equipped with F-4Fs and based at Pferdsfeld.

JaboG 36 has some 46 Phantoms on strength.

JG 71 carries the famous Richthofen badge on its F-4Fs.

JG 74 is named after World War II ace Werner Molders.

AG 51 'Immelmann' provides all-weather recce via RF-4Es.

AG 52, sister unit to AG 51, also has RF-4Es.

JaboG 31 'Boelcke' has Tornados at Norvenich.

JaboG 32, also a Tornado unit, flies from Lechfield.

JaboG 33 is a third fighter-bomber unit with Tornados.

Tornados in the strike role. Each aircraft in the wing carries the unit emblem (a diving eagle over the sea) at the top of each side of the fin. The other combat unit is MFG 2 at Eggebek, whose anti-shipping Tornadoes became operational in September 1986; the unit badge is a figure 2 on a gunsight marking. The Atlantics are based at Nordholz and have codes from 61 + 01 to 61 + 20. Neither they nor the helicopters operated by MFG 5 at Kiel carried their unit badges at the time of writing.

Left: MarinefliegerGeschwader 5 based at Kiel operates Lynx ASW helicopters, of which 83 + 02, seen here 'dunking' its sonar, was the second machine of an order for 14. The national markings can just be seen on top of the rotor housing and the word MARINE is carried in black on the rear tail boom. MFG 5 also uses Sea Kings and Do28s.

Ghana

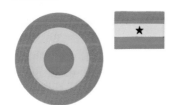

The only combat unit in the Ghanian Air Force is equipped with nine Aermacchi MB.326F/Ks, supplemented by two MB.339As. Finished in disruptive camouflage and delivered with broad yellow bands around the rear fuselage, MB.326 serials run from G.700 to G.713. Serviceability is however poor, and five have been lost since they were first delivered. Eight L-29 Delfins were received from Nigeria during 1988/89, replacement with new aircraft being out of the question for budgetary reasons. GAF aircraft all carry three-digit serials prefixed G (other types in use are F.27 Friendships, BN-2A Islanders and Short Skyvan transports.) National roundels and fin flashes are applied in the usual positions.

Greece

The Hellenic Air Force, or Elliniki Aeroporia, operates an odd mixture of Western combat aircraft, the most modern of which are 40 Dassault Mirage 2000EG/BGs and an equal number of F-16C/Ds.

Also in front line service are 33 Mirage F.1Cs used in the interception role; 50 A-7H/TA-7H Corsairs, 94 F-104G Starfighters, 60 or more F-4E/RF-4E Phantoms, and 90 F-5A/NF-5A Freedom Fighters. In addition, many surplus aircraft have been offered to the HAF by NATO allies, including 28 ex-USAF F-4Es, 36 ex-USN A-7E/TA-7Cs, 18 ex-Luftwaffe RF-4Es, a number of AlphaJets and a dozen Dutch NF-5As. In addition, a further order for 20 F-16C/Ds is in prospect. ►

The fixed-wing transport fleet is about 50 strong, and aircraft types include the C-130H Hercules, NAMC YS-11, Do-28 Skyservant and C-47 Dakota.

The Greek national insignia roundel is applied to the wings and fuselage with the vertical markings on the fin. There is no standard type of camouflage on HAF aircraft, the Starfighters and Phantoms retaining the US Vietnam-style two-greens- and-brown scheme, the Mirages have a light blue/grey scheme and F-16s retain the standard two-tone grey finish. Most of the transports, except VIP and government machines, have a disruptive camouflage.

Serial numbers on HAF aircraft take the form of the machine's construction number or, if the aircraft had a previous identity when it was acquired by the service from another operator, that number retained and painted on the fin. An F-104G, built as 63-12720, went to the Spanish Air Force and was then transferred to the HAF as 32720. This number is carried on the fin with the additional 'buzz' marking FG-720 on the fuselage.

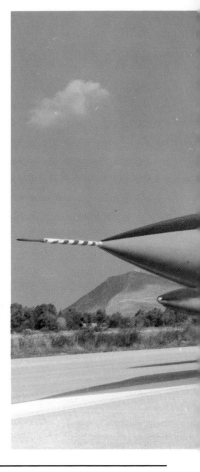

Right: Greece has received more than 50 F-104s: this example carries the fin serial 32719 plus the old US-style 'buzz' number FG-719 on the rear fuselage.

Guatemala

This Central American republic allocates only limited funds for defence purposes and operates just eleven Cessna A-37B light attack aircraft flying with the single combat squadron. These machines carry the initials FAG (Fuerza Aérea Guatemalteca) on the fin, together with the serial number (three digits ranging between 416 and 460). In addition to the A-37Bs, six PC-7 Turbo-Trainers have been given underwing armament for the attack role and seven IAI Arava transports are used in the COIN role; surviving PC-7s of the 12 machines originally delivered are retained for use at the pilot training school.

The five-pointed white star on a blue disc is usually painted on the wings and fuselage with the tail marking applied on the fin or, in the case of larger aircraft such as the DC-3 and Arava, as vertical stripes the full width of the rudder in common with other Latin American air forces. Some transports carry FUERZA AEREA GUATEMALTECA along the cabin top.

Guinea Republic

The pan-African colours carried on aircraft of the Force Aérienne de Guinée duplicate those used by Ghana, Togo and the Congo, though in the latter case the design is more elaborate; Mali, Rwanda, and Senegambia also use these colours, though their air arms are too small to warrant inclusion in this book. Confirmation of their application on the eight MiG-17 fighter-bombers supplied by the Soviet Union some years ago has yet to come to light due to the almost total lack of pictures from this country. It seems unlikely that the survivors of the MiG-17 fleet and the two MiG-15UTI Midgets are still flyable, but three or four MiG-21s were supplied by Russia in return for landing rights, and there have been unconfirmed reports of a small number of MiG-19s in service. The transport fleet consists of a single An-12 Cub, one or two IL-18 Coots and four An-14 Clods, while four helicopters, a Romanian supplied Puma and one each of French Gazelle, Ecureuil and Alouette III, remain in the inventory.

Haiti

The only French-speaking republic in Central America, Haiti failed to take advantage of the coup in which the dictator, Jean-Claude Duvalier, otherwise known as Baby Doc, was overthrown. A counter coup in 1990 saw a military dictatorship installed, and the fortunes of the Corps d'Aviation d'Haiti have gone from bad to worse. Four S.211 trainers, the only jet aircraft in the inventory, were sold in April 1990, leaving only eight Cessna 337(O-2) Super Skymasters, converted for the COIN mission with underwing hardpoints, as force proejectors, supplemented by four SF-260TP armed trainers. The national insignia shows strong US influence, reflecting the fact that initial help and equipment came from the American Government.

Honduras

The national marking applied to aircraft of the Fuerza Aérea Hondurena takes one of the five stars from the Honduran flag and locates it between the blue bars, horizontally across the rudder. For the wing marking both roundels and blue-white-blue tips have been used. The main combat element is 12 F-5E/F Tiger IIs supplied by the USA in 1987/88, while 15 A-37B Dragonflies from the same source fly the light attack mission. The status of 12 Super Mystere B.2s and 10 F-86E/F/K Sabres is currently uncertain. As with most Latin American air arms, the service initials (FAH) are applied to the fins of most aircraft together with the serial number, which takes the form of three or, in the case of the A-37Bs four digits.

Hungary

On the dissolution of the Warsaw Pact in April 1990, the Magyar Legiero changed its name to Magyar Honvedseg Repulo Csapatai and is reportedly planning to drop the red star from its national insignia, replacing it with a chevron in red, white, and green. MiG-23MF Flogger Bs are operated in the air defence role, painted in air superiority grey, while the 80 plus MiG-21 Fishbeds mainly carry brown/grey camouflage, as do Su-22M Fitters and Su-25 Frogfoot, in the interdiction and close air support roles respectively. Mi-24 Hind assault helicopters were originally delivered in grey/green camouflage, but this was replaced by a green/light green scheme. In 1989 a dark green/earth brown paint job appeared on Hinds and Hips.

India

In terms of numbers of aircraft, the Indian Air force is among the world's largest air arms with nearly 2,000 aircraft in service. Since July 1947, when India gained independence, it has been engaged in four conflicts, and most recently aided government forces in Sri Lanka. In an effort to provide a modern effective air force, a major re-equipment programme has been underway for many years, and is continuing in 1992. The Indian Air Force and Navy operate a mix of Russian and Western (but very few American) types.

A consistent theme in Indian procurement is the desire to manufacture their own combat aircraft. Jaguars and MiG-27 Flogger Js are built under licence by Indian industry, while the newly acquired MiG-29s are assembled from Russian supplied 'knocked-down' kits.

The Indian roundel of saffron, white and green is carried on the fuselage, usually on the nose, and on top and bottom surfaces of the wings. The fin flash, with green foremost on both sides, varies in size and position according to aircraft type: some, such as the MiG-23BN, have it near the top of the fin, while ▶

Left: A Jaguar belonging to 14 Sqn. the first Indian unit to achieve operational status with the type. The Jaguar is known as the *Shamser* in Indian service and this is probably one of the 18 machines initially lent to India from RAF stocks to help achieve IOC quickly.

the Jaguars have a broad marking aligned with the top line of the fuselage. However, in all cases the aircraft serial number is positioned above the marking, usually in black. The number is also carried under the wings.

Indian Air Force serials are allocated in blocks with a role prefix. Three or four numbers form each serial, but for security reasons the IAF leaves groups of numbers out of the blocks, making strength assessment difficult. Even the role prefixes of a particular aircraft type change. As an aid to type identification, some recent prefix letters and representative serials are listed in the table at the foot of the page.

Squadron badges
Squadron badges are applied to some aircraft, usually to the nose or forward fuselage area. Examples are 47 Sqn (MiG-29s) with a black and white stylised archer on a yellow disc on the forward intake trunking, 14 Sqn (Jaguars) with red and yellow chequers on the intake side, 37 Sqn (MiG-21s) with a black panther in a white disc, and 5 Sqn (Jaguars) with an elephant on a white or yellow disc on the forward fuselage.

IAF colour schemes are wide-ranging, with Fulcrums and Mirage 2000s wearing two-tone grey or blue air superiority colours, while the attack squadrons have aircraft in different disruptive schemes — green/grey on the Jaguars and at least two different patterns of green/brown/tan on the MiG-23s. Some MiG-21s are sprayed in darker shades of green and grey than those used on the Jaguars, though it would appear from photographs that colours are subject to frequent changes. This is apparent even on aircraft which have been in service no more than a few months, and must be at least partly attributable to the violent extremes of climate to which the aircraft are subject both in flight and when parked in the open on airfields.

Naval Aviation
Aircraft operated by the Navy carry the legend NAVY or INDIAN NAVY and have serials beginning with IN followed by three digits. Sea Harriers of 300 Sqn carry serials from IN601 and a leaping white tiger insignia across the fin as the unit badge; colour scheme of these aircraft is dark grey and white.

Other types in service include Alizé ASW aircraft based aboard INS *Viraat* and INS *Vikrant*, and carrying serials in the IN201 range; Islanders; Ilyushin Il-38 patrol aircraft; Kamov Ka-25 Hormone ASW helicopters; and Alouette III *Chetak* liaison and transport helicopters.

Indian prefixes and representative serials

BA	Hawker Hunter F.56	BA201-	Advanced Training
BH	Hawker Siddeley HS.748	BH572-	Used as tactical freighters and trainers
BL	Antonov An-12 'Cub'	BL532-	Being replaced by Il-76
C	MiG-21FL/M/MF/bis	C448-	About 400 in service
HM	Dornier Do228	HM667-	Light transport
IF	BAC Canberra B(I).8/PR.57	IF895-	Few remaining mainly for reconnaissance
JM	Jaguar 1M	JM251-	Maritime attack
JS	SEPECAT Jaguar	JS101-	Production continues
JT	SEPECAT Jaguar	JT051-	Two-seat trainers (Jaguar known as *Shamsher* in IAF)
K	Ilyushin Il-76 'Candid'	K2661-	Known as *Gajaraj* in IAF
K	Antonov An-32 'Cline'	K2668-	Known as *Sutlej* in IAF
KB	MiG-29 Fulcrum	KB701-	Air superiority fighter
KF	Dassault Mirage 2000H	KF101-	39 in service *Vajra* in IAF service
KT	Dassault Mirage 2000TH	KT201-	Seven in service
SM	MiG-23BN 'Flogger'	SM201-	Ground-support aircraft
TS	MiG-27M 'Flogger'	TS501-	Replaced *Ajeet*
U	MiG-21U 'Mongol'	U655-	Two-seat trainer

Indonesia

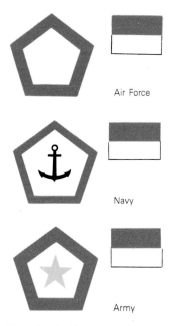

Air Force

Navy

Army

The red and white pentagon marking was adopted for Indonesian military aircraft following the country's achievement of independence from the Netherlands after World War II; the colours are traditional and date back to the 13th century Majapahit Empire. Aircraft operated by the National Armed Forces — Air Force, or Tentara Nasional Indonesia — Angkatan Udara (TNI-AU), carry the marking on wings and fuselage with a red and white flash on the fin.

The combat element of the Indonesian Air Force comprises five squadrons. The General Dynamics F-16A/B, of which 12 have been delivered, is the most modern fighter in service, while 15 Northrop F-5E/F Tiger IIs make up the fighter complement. Two squadrons operate Douglas A-4E/TA-4H Skyhawks in the attack role. The fifth combat squadron is equipped with Rockwell OV-10F Broncos.

Serials are issued in blocks and when applied to aircraft are given prefix letters indicating the machine's specific role. Examples are: TS for fighters, used on the F-5Es (TS-0501-0512); TT for attack aircraft such as the A-4E (TT-0401-); LL for the Hawk advanced trainers (LL-5301-); and HH for helicopters, applied to Bö105Cs (HH-1501-). ▶

Below: An Indonesian Hawk with national markings on the port wing, fuselage and fin.

Indonesian Naval Aviation

GAF Nomads and Searchmasters, Nurtanio-built Bö105Cs and Super Pumas form the bulk of the Tentara Nasional Indonesia — Angatan Laut. Their task is short-range coastal patrol among the country's hundreds of islands to help contain the recent increase in piracy. All TNI-AL aircraft carry the national marking with an anchor symbol in the centre and a prominent serial — usually in black — on the fin. Army aircraft of the TNI-AD (the suffix standing for Angkatan Dorat) are identified by a yellow star in the centre of the national red pentagon markings.

Iran

The eight year war of attrition against neighbouring Iraq, which ended in August 1988 with no significant advantages gained by either side, left the Islamic Republic of Iran Air Force, once the best equipped in the region, sadly depleted, partly by operational losses and partly by the need to cannibalize aircraft for spares which could not be obtained by other means. The remarkable thing was that they maintained an air presence at all in the later stages of what was then known as the Gulf War.

Of the original 79 F-14A Tomcats, only about twenty are believed to be flyable, while the serviceability of the radars and avionics of these few is, to say the least, dubious. The F-4 Phantom fleet, once over 200 strong, has been reduced to less than 50, while less than half of the original 169 F-5E/Fs are still flyable. Small numbers of Xian F-7s and Shenyang F-6s have reportedly been delivered by China, but confirmation of this is lacking. The only new fighters to definitely arrive in recent years were 14 MiG-29 Fulcrums during 1990.

Disruptive 'spinach and sand' camouflage schemes are still widely used, while the national insignia remains the same as in Imperial days, although IRIAF has replaced the original IIAF. Serial numbers are carried on the fin, allocated in blocks and consisting of up to six digits. Phantoms carry numbers 3-601, 602, 603 etc, while the F-14 numbers run from 3-6001 to 3-6077. Little is known of current unit markings, which formerly were widely carried. It is believed that some Iraqi aircraft which defected to Iran during the Gulf War of 1991 have been impressed into Iranian service, but again, reliable information is scanty.

Iraq

The numerically strong and well equipped Al Quwwat al Jawwiya al Iraqiya (Iraqi Air Force) failed to achieve decisive results in the eight year war against Iran and was then decimated by Desert Storm operations early in 1991. Over 100 Iraqi aircraft escaped to Iran, where they were impounded, while many were destroyed by Allied air power.

The triangular insignia and the fin flash have the same colours as the national flag — red for courage in battle, white for generosity, black for the era of Caliphates and past glory and green for the Islamic prophet Mohammed. Iraqi serial numbers are applied to the fin: older aircraft generally carry three-digit numbers, while later types such as the Mirages and Su-20s are in the ranges of 4000 and 1100 respectively.

Ireland (Eire)

The Celtic boss marking in its present form was adopted after the Second World War, the three colours from the national flag symbolizing the green countryside and Catholic people along with orange for the Protestants of Ulster in the north and white for the desire for peace between the two communities. It is carried on the wings and fuselage of the 11 dark green camouflaged SF.260

Warriors used for training and counter-insurgency duties, the six natural metal CM170 Magisters and the six green Cessna 172 Rockets. Three CN-235s have been ordered for the maritime reconnaissance role. The only other prominent marking is the individual aircraft number, comprising three digits and painted in white on the fuselage of the dark-finished machines and in black on the natural metal aircraft. The current allocations are as shown in the table below.

In addition to the circular national markings, some Alouette IIIs have had large tricolour flags painted on the rear fuselage to clarify the operator during anti-terrorist border patrol duties.

Irish Air Corps serial numbers

SIAI-Marchetti SF.260WE Warrior	222, 223, 225-231, 235
Fouga CM170 Magister	215-220
Cessna FR172H/K Rocket	203, 205, 206, 208-210
Aérospatiale SA.316 Alouette III	195-197, 202, 211-214
Aérospatiale SA.342L Gazelle	237, 241
Aérospatiale SA.365F Dauphin	244-248

Israel

One of the most combat-capable air arms in the world, the Israeli Air Force or Heyl Ha'Avir is also one of the most security conscious. Formed in 1948 following the declaration of independence for the State of Israel, this comparatively small force has fought and won three major wars against its Arab neighbours. To the Israelis, one lost war will be the last war.

Israel's national marking is modelled on the Zionist 'shield of David' symbol. On a white background, it has remained prominent on IAF aircraft engaged in front-line and support operations, located on both

sides of the fuselage and top and bottom surfaces of both wings. The exception to this practice is the F-16, of which 71 of the original A/B batch survive, augmented by 135 F-16C/Ds. On these machines, the wing-fuselage blending has meant that no fuselage insignia is carried, national indentification being by means of the 25in (63.5cm) wing markings. To date, all the F-16s noted have employed a disruptive camouflage for the attack role (officially designated FS 33531 sand, FS 30219 tan, and FS 34424 grey/green), with FS 36375 Compass Gray on the underside, as have the suriviving 110 or so F-4E Phantoms and the similar number of A-4 Skyhawks, although both types employ green as an additional colour over the top surfaces. The other major combat type is the F-15 Eagle interceptor of which 77 are in service. Many Kfirs are in storage, although four squadrons still operate this indigenously developed aircraft. ▶

**Above: Two F-15 Eagles of the
Israel Defence Force/Air Force
prepare for take-off.**

**Above: 'Skyblazer' in Hebrew on
the nose of F-15 No 657 is
accompanied by four Arab 'kill'
markings. A number of
individually marked Eagles equip
one of the IAF units.**

**Right: The F-15s equipping the
unit noted above carry the tail
insignia seen here, the black and
white marking being applied to
the inside of the fins. Aircraft 644
is named 'Lightning' while
another machine called
'Gunman' sports two 'kills' and
has the fin number 678, plus the
two Eagle motifs. The countershaded greys are shown to good
effect in the lower illustration.**

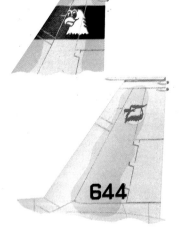

The other official marking applied
to IAF aircraft are the individual
numbers applied in black on the fin
and on the nosewheel door for
ground maintenance use. These
three-digit numbers bear no relation
to the construction number and are
not applied in batch sequences,
there being numerous gaps intended
to confuse enemy intelligence as to
the exact IAF operational strength at
any given time. For example, the 67
F-16As delivered (incidentally, these
were ferried to Israel carrying USAF
markings) carry numbers ranging
from 100 to 298 and it is quite possible that, periodically, the numbers
are changed between aircraft. It is
also worth recording that as a further
aid to security the same numbers are
regularly carried by different aircraft
types.

Above: A subtle two-tone grey scheme is carried by this Kfir-C7 fighter-bomber as it taxis out for a mission from a base in the Negev desert. The fuel tanks are still in the old colours.

Right: Tail unit of Kfir-C2 987 in air defence grey. The censoring of tail badges by the Israeli Defence Ministry has been less stringent in recent years, but accurate squadron number tie-ups remain elusive.

Above: 'Cafe au lait' is the Israeli nickname for this form of desert camouflage evolved for the low-level attack role. IAF fin numbers are known to change, preventing strength assessment.

Israeli Air Force unit badges have been a source of fascination since the 1960s, when the first American equipment joined the squadrons. Any pictures emanating from the IAF or taken by jouranlists were only released so long as these particular markings were censored. Such was the regular censorship of these badges that some enthusiasts wondered if in fact there were any markings there in the first place. A more relaxed attitude in recent years has seen a considerable number of markings released, although linking these to specific units is still rather theoretical. Examples are F-16Cs with what appears to be a stylised

MiG-21 in a red circle surmounting a silver lightning flash, and F-15s with black/white eagles heads.

In addition to the badges, which are usually located near the top of the fin, some aircraft have been seen with red and white or blue and white striped or plain red rudders. Coloured fin flashes (in red) have been noted on Phantoms, a type which has also appeared sporting 'sharks teeth' around the nose. While the IAF has given little publicity to its 'aces' during recent wars, a number of aircraft have been displayed carrying various miniature Arab roundels on the nose, the highest number to date being 13 applied to the nose of a Mirage III. ▶

Eagles have also been shown carrying nicknames in Hebrew, such as 'Gunman' coded 678 with two kills on the nose and cartoon eagles painted on both sides of the vertical fins. Others are 'Skyblazer' with four kills and 'Typhoon' with two kills and the fin number 658.

The Phantom fleet is still a major attack force, with over 120 in the inventory, and many F-4Es are scheduled to undergo upgrading to Kurnass 2000 standards, with greatly improved avionics. The first of these, number 668, was handed over in April 1989. Also in hand is a scheme to upgrade early F-15A/Bs. Eighteen AH-64A Apache battlefield helicopters are in the course of delivery, while UH-60 Black Hawks are also on the Israeli shopping list. Wanted for the late '90s is a replacement for the IAI Tsukit (Magister) jet trainer. Currently under evaluation are Tucano, PC-9, S.211 and IA.63 Pampa.

The civil registration for Israel is 4X, but IAF transports also carry non-military registrations on their wings and fins. The C-130 Hercules range from 4X-FBA to -FBZ, while Boeing 707s flown in the tanker, elint and straight transport roles run from 4X-JYA.

The Israeli helicopter force is also mainly painted in the sand, tan and green scheme with the national star on the rear of the fuselage or the tail boom. About 30 CH-53D Sea Stallions form the core of the helicopter transport force, supplemented by 20 or so Bell 212s, a few Bell 205s and some Sikorsky S-65Cs.

Below: A two-seat F-16B, one of the first of over 200 F-16s being delivered to Israel. This aircraft has the 25in (63.5cm) national roundels under each wing. The Israelis also have a rarely-seen combat version of the two-seat F-16B, apparently modified with special equipment for the Wild Weasel defence suppression role.

Italy

The Aeronautica Militare Italiano (AMI), or Italian Air Force, assigns most of its front-line strength to NATO's 5th Allied Tactical Air Force for the defence of southern Europe. Of a total strength of some 900 aircraft about one third are combat types, namely Panavia Tornados, Lockheed/Aeritalia F-104S ASA Starfighters, and Aeritalia/Aermacchi/Ambraer AMX attack aircraft. These commenced entering service in 1989, replacing elderly F-104Gs and Fiat G-91s. Basic AMI organization consists of Stormi (Swarms), equivalent to Wings and formed by up to three Gruppi (Groups), each comprising two or three Squadriglie or Squadrons.

The basic AMI marking is the roundel in the national colours. This is positioned in the standard location of wings and fuselage and dates from its use by the Co-belligerent Air Force toward the end of World War II. No tail marking is carried.

Italian military aircraft are allocated serial numbers prefixed MM (Matricola Militare) applied in 10cm-high figures usually toward the rear of the fuselage and above or below the official aircraft designation. Some of the current range of MM serial numbers and their aircraft are given in the accompanying table. The MM serial system is applied to all types of aircraft in blocks according to role as shown.

AMI combat aircraft carry the main formation number (6 in the case of the 6th Stormo) and an individual number. These are applied on the nose or rear fuselage, either split by the roundel or hyphenated. The exceptions to this ruling are some second-line units which have prefix letters followed by the aircraft number. Current combat units can be identified from the table of units and badges (see overleaf).

Some rescue-related helicopters carry disctinctive yellow and red areas plus the abbreviation S.A.R. and the legend AERONAUTICA MILITARE. Navy-operated helicopters can be identified by the word MARINA on the rear boom and an anchor motif, while Army equipment carries the marking ESERCITO and the prefix in the style of E.I. followed by the roundel in most cases and a three-digit number. Finally, mention should be included of the Italian national aerobatic team Frecce Tricolori as one of the most brightly-painted units in the AMI. The MB.339s flown by the unit carry red, white and green colours together with dark blue gloss fuselages and large yellow numbers on the fins. They are a familiar sight at European air shows, and like most national display teams they also have a combat role, as shown by the photograph on page 14-15. ▶

MM serial blocks

MM500	Prototypes
MM5000N	Naval helicopters
MM6000	Jet fighters
MM40000	Atlantic aircraft
MM50000	Trainers and liaison aircraft
MM60000	Transports
MM80000	Helicopters
MM90000	SF.260 trainers

Current Matricola Militare serial numbers

Panavia Tornado	MM7001-MM7090	90 attack versions for AMI
Panavia Tornado	MM55000-MM55009	10 trainers
Lockheed F-104G	MM6501-MM6660	Approx 25 remain in AMI use
Aeritalia F-104S	MM6701-MM6946	140 in AMI use
Aeritalia G.91Y	MM6441-MM6960	Being replaced by AMX
Fiat G.91R	MM6265-MM6424	Being replaced by AMX
Breguet Atlantic	MM40108-MM40125	18 used for maritime patrol
Lockheed C-130H Hercules	MM61988-MM62001	12 with AMI

AMI combat units, aircraft and badges

2° Stormo	AMX	Black lancer over white cloud and blue background
3° Stormo	F-104S ASA	Two black cats' heads and two white cats' heads
4° Stormo	F-104S ASA	White rearing horse on black background
5° Stormo	F-104S ASA	Diana the Hunter drawing bow in white on black background
6° Stormo	Tornado	Red devil's head (Diavolo Rosso) on black background
8° Stormo	AMX	White angel holding a bomb on black background
9° Stormo	F-104S ASA	Black rearing horse on white background
32° Stormo	AMX	Black diving eagle on white background (sharkmouth painted on intake)
36° Stormo	Tornado/ F-104S ASA	Silver eagle on white ring and blue background
51° Stormo	F-104S ASA	Black cat chasing three green mice on white backgrounds
53° Stormo	F-104S ASA	Gold and blue scimitar on yellow background
30° Stormo	Atlantic	Purple eagle, white shark, light blue/dark blue background

Above: AMI Panavia Tornado 6-02 in the markings of the 154° Gruppo of the 6°Stormo. This unit served initially as the Italian AF's weapons training unit. The nose code indicates the unit, followed by the individual aircraft number. The famous red devil badge is on the fin, with the serial number (MM7007) in black below. 10 Italian Tornados took part in the 1991 Gulf war, with one being lost in action.

Below: The AMI received 100 Tornados, comprising 87 strike versions, 12 trainers and a single prototype, although some may be converted to the ECR Recce version. The eagle badge and yellow flash on the fin of this aircraft identifies it as a 36°Stormo machine, and the green cat badge on the intake shows that it belongs to the 156°Gruppo. Italian Tornados often carry Kormoran anti-ship missiles under the fuselage.

Ivory Coast

As an ex-French colony, the Ivory Coast adopted a flag with similar dimensions to that of France but formed of orange, white and green. A miniature of this ensign is painted on the fins of the four AlphaJets in service, the only combat aircraft currently operated by the Force Aérienne de la Côte d'Ivoire. Like other types in use, these machines carry a civil registration in black on the fin (TU-VCA to -VCG); roundels in the national colours are applied on wings and fuselage. Transport, liaison and training aircraft and helicopters have nearly all been supplied by or via France and have military markings plus registrations in the TU-VAA to TU-VZZ block.

Japan

Known as the Sun Disc and originating some 2600 years ago, the Japanese national flag is one of the simplest of designs and is carried on all military aircraft as well as on the aircraft operated by Japan Air Lines. The present design, almost unchanged from those that had gone before, was adopted by the re-formed Japanese Air Self-Defence Force (Nihon Koku Jieitai) in 1954. Initial equipment was almost wholly of US origin and with a few exceptions this situation continues today. McDonnell Douglas F-4EJ Phantoms and F-15J Eagles, the latter type having replaced Lockheed F-104J Starfighters, constitute the major portion of the air defence element protecting the Japanese islands, but these are supplemented by an indigenous design, the Mitsubishi F-1, which is a developed version of the T-2 trainer with only one seat, gun and missile armament and under-wing weapon pylons.

JASDF organisation is based on established lines, the largest operational formation being the Air Wing or Kokudan, parent unit to two squadrons or Hikotai; current aircraft holding is officially 18 per squadron although there are plans to increase this to 24. All the JASDF combat units have colourful insignia displayed on the fin. The present JASDF front-line strength is as shown in the table below.

Serial numbers on the aircraft flown by these units are located on the fin, but their composition is somewhat different from the accepted Western form. The six-figure

JASDF combat units

2 Kokudan	203 Hikotai	F-15J Eagle
	207 Hikotai	F-15J Eagle
3 Kokudan	3 Hikotai	F-1
	8 Hikotai	F-1
5 Kokudan	202 Hikotai	F-15J Eagle
	301 Hikotai	F-15J Eagle
6 Kokudan	303 Hikotai	F-4EJ Phantom
	306 Hikotai	F-4EJ Phantom
7 Kokudan	204 Hikotai	F-15J Eagle
	305 Hikotai	F-15J Eagle
8 Kokudan	304 Hikotai	F-4EJ Phantom
	6 Hikotai	F-1

serials are split into a series of individual digits, each of which has a specific meaning. The first digit indicates the year in which the aircraft was purchased; the second is the aircraft type (single- or multi-engined, jet or helicopter); the third is the basic role of the aircraft (see table); and finally the last three form the aircraft's individual, sequential number.

JASDF role numbers:

0	Trainers
1	Transports
3	Miscellaneous
4	Helicopters
5	Jet trainers
6	Reconnaissance
7	Day fighters
8	All-weather fighters

An example of the current system, which is used on all JASDF aircraft, is provided by the F-4EJ Phantom serial 57-8359:

Serial 57-8359

5	Aircraft purchased in 1975
7	Jet-powered
8	All-weather fighter
359	The 59th F-4EJ purchased, the first having been given the number 301; a total of 140 were eventually procured

The individual aircraft number is usually repeated on the nose for quick identification purposes on the ground. Maintenance and safety instructions over the airframe are ap-plied in English and Japanese though such instructions do not invariably appear in both languages.

Japanese Maritime Self-Defence Force

The Nihon Kaiyo Jieitai (Japanese Maritime Self-Defence Force) has no pure combat aircraft, but does have an effective collection of ASW aircraft and helicopters. Lockheed P-3C Orions are replacing the turboprop-powered P2V-7 Neptunes for long-range patrol, while PS-1 flying boats provide valuable ASW support. Mitsubishi-built Sikorsky HSS-2 Sea Kings and SH-60J Sea Hawks are operated from both ships and shore bases.

JMSDF types employ an identification system similar to that of the Air Force, but shorter. The initial figure indicates the type and the other three the individual aircraft number. The key to the present code is as shown.

JMSDF role numbers

2	Single-engined ASW
4	Twin-engined ASW
5	Four-engined ASW
6	Trainers
7	Communications/trainers
8	Helicopters
9	Utility/liaison types

Kawasaki-built P-3C Orion 5015 carries the initial number indicating a four-engined ASW aircraft and subsequent figures denoting the 15th machine of its type in JMSDF ▶

Below: A JASDF F-15J of the 203rd Hikotai, belonging to the 2nd Kokudan, based at Chitose. The alternate view shows the tail badge of the 202nd Hikotai.

Left: The red disc on this F-15J Eagle is partially obscured by the movable air intake as the pilot prepares for take-off. Some 187 Eagles have been ordered by the Japanese Air Self-Defence Force, most of them manufactured locally.

Below Left: This F-4EJ belonged to the 305th Hikotai which has since re-equipped with F-15Js. Over 100 of these tough multi-role fighters in Japanese service are due to be updated to keep them effective well into the next century.

service. The aircraft number is repeated on the nose. Unit badges are carried on the fins of most fixed-wing aircraft and the title of the operating arm is painted on the rear fuselage of all types in Japanese characters.

Japanese Ground Self-Defence Force

The Japanese Ground Self-Defence Force (Nihon Rikujyo Jieitai) is principally a support force for the ground armies, of which there are five stationed across the Japanese islands. Only Bell AH-1J HueyCobras have an offensive support capability among the types in use, these being armed with cannon and TOW missiles. JGSDF aircraft carry five-number serials, of which the last four digits are normally displayed large on the fin; the full serial is often marked near the nose. The initial digit indicates the machine's primary role and the last four identify the individual machine of the series.

JGSDF role numbers

1	Fixed-wing liaison/observation
2	Fixed-wing miscellaneous
3	Observation helicopters
4	Light transport helicopters
5	Medium transport helicopters
6	Basic trainers
7	Tactical support helicopters
8	Primary trainers

Arm of Service is indicated in Japanese characters on each side of the fuselage, and serial numbers are prefixed JG.

Jordan

Dassault-Breguet Mirage F.1EJ/CJs and Northrop F-5Es form the defensive front-line force in the Royal Jordanian Air Force (Al Quwwat al Jawwiya al Malakiya al Urduniya). Some older F-5As have been disposed of, while attempts to procure Mirage 2000s and Tornados have failed. Twenty-four Bell UH-1F Cobra attack helicopters serve in the anti-tank role, while two SH-60 Black Hawks and 11 Super Pumas are the most recent additions to the rotary wing transport fleet. The national roundel incorporates the seven-pointed star representing the first seven verses of the Koran while the fin flash has the same colours as the roundel with the white star on red leading on each side. Individual aircraft numbers are applied on the fuselage sides in Arabic style, although C-130 Hercules transports carry standard Western numerals both on the nose and fin. The Hercules also have the title ROYAL JORDANIAN AIR FORCE

Kenya

Known as the '82 Air Force following an attempted coup by Kenya Air Force officers in 1982, the air arm is under the control of the Army but the national insignia is retained, as is the fin flash. Air defence is the responsibility of a squadron of Northrop F-5Es. Twelve Hawk 52s double in the attack/advanced training role, supplemented by the remaining five Strikemasters, while a dozen Tucano 51s are in the course of delivery in early 1992.

Aircraft serials are carried on the fuselage with the last two numbers applied large at the top of the fin. Up to four digits are used, with blocks

Korea (North)

Established in 1948 as a socialist country, the Democratic People's Republic of Korea exists behind almost closed borders, releasing little information about its armed forces. The Korean People's Army Air Force operates aircraft obtained from Russia and China. Current equipment

behind the cockpit. The civil registration prefix JY followed by another three letters is carried on the Bulldog trainers operated by the RJAF's Air Academy at the King Abdullah base, Amman.

Above: Jordan is one of more than 30 countries to operate the Northrop F-5. This F-5E has the serial number on the fin and miniaturized national markings wings and intakes.

Kenya Air Force serial blocks

100	Light transports (Dornier Do28D-2 Skyservant)
200	Transports (DHC-8 -100 Dash 8)
300	Liaison aircraft
400	Transport helicopters (Aérospatiale Puma)
500	Light helicopters (Hughes 500M Scout/500MD Defender)
600	Light attack jets (BAC Strikemaster Mk 87)
700	Trainers (Scottish Aviation Bulldog 103/127)
800	Not allocated
900	Fighters (Northrop F-5E/F)
1000	Jet trainers (BAe Hawk Mk 52)

allocated as shown.

A total of 48 MD.500s have been acquired for anti-tank, COIN and civil support roles, eight of them MD.500MGs equipped with searchlights for anti-poacher patrols.

includes about 30 MiG-29 Fulcrums, 58 MiG-23 Floggers and over 150 MiG-21PF/PFMA Fishbeds in the interceptor role. Large numbers of F-6 Farmers remain on strength. The attack mission is mainly flown by about 40 A-5 Fantans, backed by large numbers of MiG-17 Frescos, and a single unit of Su-7BMK Fitters. Close air support is the responsibility of a single unit of Su-25 Frogfoot.

North Korean aircraft carry the national roundel on wings and fuselage and have individual numbers marked prominently on noses, engine cowlings or nacelles. MiG-21s have carried three-digit numbers in the 200 series, while Antonov An-24 transports have been noted in the 500 series.

Korea (South)

Occupying the southern part of the Korean peninsula up to the 38th parallel, the Republic of Korea is supported by the United States in a shaky truce with its North Korean neighbour. The Republic of Korea Air Force (ROKAF), or Han-guk Kong Goon, is almost totally equipped with aircraft of US origin and even the fledgling aircraft industry set up in the late 1970s produces American designs. F-16C/Ds are the mainstay of the ROKAF fighter force, with orders totalling 159 to date, supplementing 123 F-4D/E Phantoms and 199 F-5E/F Tiger IIs.

The ROKAF insignia is the classic Yin/Yang, symbolising balance, in red and blue, the two divided by a thin white line, with a USA-style bar added to show alliance with that country. The abbreviation ROKAF is carried on most combat aircraft and individual machines are identified by the last three digits of the serial number. These are displayed in a larger size on the fin and also on the nosewheel door of the Phantoms in service, if not the other types. Unit bagdes are not displayed for security reasons, the only other markings being the safety and maintenance stencilling which is in both English and Korean. Camouflage employed on the F-5s and Phantoms is the standard US SE Asia two-greens-and-a- brown disruptive scheme.

Photographs of the first F-16D for South Korea, released in the spring of 1986, showed the aircraft in a three-tone grey camouflage scheme with the letters ROKAF and the serial 84-370 on the fin in a shade approximating to the Middle Grey of the radome. A low-visibility version of the national insignia was carried on the wings and aft fuselage, and rescue and maintenance stencilling was also in low-visibility form.

Kuwait

The Iraqi invasion of Kuwait in August 1990 over-ran the country very quickly, and the surviving aircraft of the Al Quwwat al Jawwiya al Kuwaitiya, mainly Mirage F.1s and Skyhawks, were evacuated to Saudi Arabia, where they became the Free Kuwaiti Air Force and flew intensively in the subsequent Desert Storm operation.

Current equipment includes 15 Mirage F.1CK/BKs, 19 A-4KU Skyhawks, and six BAe Hawk 64s. The first of 40 McDonnell Douglas F/A-18C/D Hornets was handed over in October 1991, and six arrived in Kuwait in January 1992. Final delivery is scheduled for September 1993. Sixteen Shorts Tucanos are also on order. Desert camouflage is carried by all front-line types (Sand, Light Brown and Grey on the Hawks and light and medium grey on the Hornets) and a three-digit serial on the nose in standard figures and on the tail in Arabic scripts forms the identifying mark on each aircraft. Examples are given below.

Kuwait Air Force serial numbers

140, 141 etc	BAe Hawk Mk 64
501, 502 etc	Aérspatiale SA.342K Gazelle
551, 552 etc	Aérospatiale SA.330F Puma
701, 702 etc	Dassault-Breguet Mirage F.1CK
801, 802 etc	McDonnell Douglas A-4KU Skyhawk

Laos

With the exception of a handful of transports, all equipment of the Air Force of the People's Liberation Army is of Russian origin. The sole combat element consists of about 40 MiG-21PF Fishbeds, deployed in two squadrons based at Wattay (Vientiane). Russian transport aircraft, Colts, Cokes, Curls and Codlings, are operated jointly with the national airline. Markings information is scarce with photographic evidence of current insignia almost non-existent. National markings are presumed to be carried in the usual places

Lebanon

Almost totally ineffective as a combat force, the Al Quwwat al Jawwiya al Lubnaniya operates just five Hunter F.70s and a T.66C trainer. Five each Magisters and Bulldogs fill the training role, and a single Shrike Commander acts as a VIP transport/liaison aircraft. About 38 helicopters, mainly Pumas and Alouettes, and including seven Gazelles in the anti-tank role, continue to operate. Markings are applied in the standard positions and aircraft carry three-number codes prefixed or suffixed with the letter L. The serial on the port side of the fuselage is normally applied in Arabic figures.

Libya

The plain green marking carried on aircraft of Al Quwwat al Jawwiya al Arabiya al Libyya has become a familiar emblem to US Navy aircrew in re- ▶

Below: Mirage F.1ED photographed by a US Navy aircraft off the coast of Libya.

cent years. USN carrier exercises in the Gulf of Sidra have received constant attention from Libyan aircraft, notably Mirage F.1s, MiG-23s and 25s, and two armed clashes have occurred, both involving USN F-14s. In August 1981, two Su-22 Fitters were shot down, and in what almost amounted to an action replay, two MiG-23 Floggers were destroyed on 4 January 1989. On paper the LAF is impressive, with more than 500 combat aircraft in service, but its true status and operational capability is considerably reduced from that figure. Aircrew are Syrian, Pakistani, North Korean and Palestinian.

The green insignia was adopted following Libya's protest at the visit by President Sadat of Egypt to Israel in 1977, replacing the red, white and black colours that Libya previously shared with Egypt. Aircraft are identified individually by numbers displayed on the fin and nose, sometimes in Arabic form on one side and in conventional form on the other. Three or four digits are usually involved, sometimes reflecting the aircraft serial number but no unit badges are carried. Unusually, some MiG-25s carry two sets of numbers, one example having 499 on fins and intakes plus 1035 on the nose.

Malagasy Republic

Adopted in 1959, the national flag's three colours signify sovereignty (red), purity (white) and hope (green), the insignia being applied to the fins of the MiG-21s equipping the island's sole fighter squadron. The air arm is known as l'Armée de l'Air Malgache, signifying its previous French connections. Non-combat and transport types carry a civil registration with the prefix 5R-.

Malaysia

The attractive 14-point yellow sun in Malaysia's national insignia represents the 13 states plus the capital territory Kuala Lumpur which constitute the federation. Applied until recently within a blue square; this marking is becoming more common in miniature roundel style on wings and fuselage of aircraft flown by the Royal Malaysian Air Force, or Tentera Udara Diraja Malaysia. The difficult task of defending the country, particularly the capital city, is the responsibility of Nos 11 and 12 Squadrons, equipped with Northrop F-5E/Fs,

based at Butterworth. These aircraft remain uncamouflaged with identification serials displayed on the fin in the sequence M29-01, M29-02, M29-03 etc, and like many RMAF aircraft they carry the abbreviation TUDM above the serial. Four F-5F two-seat trainers are serialled M29-15 to M29-18. Note that the RMAF reserialled their aircraft in the early 1980s; the previous style was an FM (Federation of Malaysia) prefix followed by a four-digit number, but by 1986 most aircraft had changed to the new system.

Thirty seven of the original 40 ex-USN Skyhawks remain in service with Nos 6 and 9 Squadrons, designated A-4PTM (Peculiar to Malaysia), and have a disruptive green and brown camouflage with serials beginning M32-01, M32-02, M32-03 and so on. In 1988 12 Tornadoes were ordered, but in 1990 these were cancelled and an order placed for a mixed bag of 28 BAe Hawk 100/200s.

Other types in service include C-130H Hercules transports serialled M30-01 etc, plus three patrol versions which carry the legend MARITIM on the fuselage sides; DHC-4 Caribou (M21-01 etc); S-61A Nuri (M23); Alouette III (M20); PC-7 Turbo Trainer (M33); and MB-339A (M34). Most markings are in English, but some stencilling is displayed in Bahasa Malay such as BAHAYA (Danger) and JANGAN TARK ATAU TOLAK (Do not pull or push).

Below: One of the 37 ex-USN A-4L Skyhawks refurbished for the Malaysian Air Force. Markings are minimal, with no tail flash or underwing roundels, and hardly any maintenance or emergency stencilling. Note the abbreviation TUDM for Tentera Udara Diraja Malaysia on the fin above the serial number.

Mauritania

The national marking of this West African country reflects the Muslim religion of its people. A poor economy has prevented any major expansion of the armed forces and they have now withdrawn from the Polisario-claimed area on the Moroccan border. The Force Aerienne Islamique de Mauritanie operates five armed Britten Norman BN-2A Defenders and four Cessna FTB-337G/Fs for border patrol and COIN, while two PA-31 Cheyenne IIs fly coastal patrol missions. Four MD-500Ms are used for liaison. Almost all FAIM aircraft carry civil registrations within the block 5T-MAA to -MZZ reserved for military machines; commercial aircraft run from 5T-CAA. The national marking is carried on wings and fuselage.

Mexico

The triangular marking applied to aircraft of the Fuerza Aérea Mexicana was first adopted in 1925 and comprises the national colours symbolizing hope (green), peace (white) and unity (red). Applied to wings and fuselage, it is supplemented by rudder stripes in the three colours. Combat squadrons are No 401 with F-5E/F Tiger IIs, No 202 with AT-33s, and Nos 201, 203, 204, 205, 206 and 207 with armed Pilatus PC-7 Turbo-Trainers. The original ten F-5Es, of which nine remain, were serialled 4001-4010. The AT-33s number a total of more than 30, due to deliveries of ex-USAF aircraft in 1986 and 1988, while 75 PC-7s operate in the COIN role, backed by a further ten trainers. FAM serials are assigned in four- or five-digit blocks often

Mongolia

A single squadron of MiG-21MF Fishbed interceptors about 12 strong, is the front line of air defence for the Air Force of the Mongolian People's Republic, supplemented by an equal number of obsolete MiG-17 Frescos in the attack role.

Controlled by the army, the air force has always been organised along the lines of the now defunct Soviet Union. The transport element consists of six An-24 Cokes, one An-26 Curl, and about 25 An-2 Colt biplanes, supplemented by about 12 Mi-8 Hip and Mi-4 Hound helicopters.

Morocco

The war in the Western Sahara against the Polisario guerrilla movement has had a deleterious effect on the Moroccan economy, but King Hassan remains determined never to concede the disputed territory. This has resulted in a steady arms buying programme which has seen the influx of military aircraft and ground forces equipment from a variety of countries to maintain Morocco's fighting capability. The Royal Moroccan Air Force or Al Quwwat al Jawiya al Malakiya Marakishiya operates 39 Dassault-Breguet

Mexican Air Force role prefixes

AP	Avión Presidencial
BR	Búsqueda y Rescate (Search and Rescue)
BRE	Búsqueda, Reconocimento y Escuela (Search, Reconnaissance and Training)
EAP	Entrenador Avanzado Pilatus (PC-7 advanced trainers)
EBA	Entrenador Beechcraft Avanzado (Beech Bonanza Advanced Trainers)
EBP	Entrenador Beechcraft Primario (Beech Musketeer primary trainers)
ETL	Escuadron de Transporte Ligero (Light Transport Squadron)
ETM	Escuadron de Transporte Mediano (Medium Transport Squadron)
ETP	Escuadron de Transporte Pesado (Heavy Transport Squadron)
HBRB	Helicoptero de Búsqueda y Rescate Bell (applied to Bell 212 rescue helicopters)
JE	Jet Entrenador (Jet Trainer)
JP	Jet de Pelea (Jet Fighter)
TEB/D/P	Transporte Ejecutivo Beechcraft/Douglas/Piper (Executive Transports)
TP	Transport Presidencial (Presidential Transport)

unrelated to manfuacturers' construction numbers. Normally applied on the aircraft fin, the number is usually prefixed by one or more letters. Those most likely to be noted are shown in the table.

Naval aircraft

Mexican Navy aircraft usually carry the legend ARMADA DE MEXICO, an anchor insignia plus the standard national marking. Serial prefixes include HMR for Naval Rescue Helicopter, ME Naval Trainer, MP Naval Patrol (14 Grumman HU-16 Albatross at several bases), MT Naval Transport and MU Naval Utility. As with FAM aircraft, the serial and triangular marking are also applied under the wings.

Mirage F.1s (25 dual-role F.1EH and 25 F.1CH interceptors), plus 24 Northrop F-5E/F fighter-bombers. Both these types operate in disruptive desert camouflage and carry the national markings on wings and fuselage. The tail flash is formed of a pentagram, or Solomon's Seal emblem, on a red background at the top of the rudder in the case of the Mirages, and located centrally on the fin of the F-5s. As part of the US aid package which included the F-5s, six OV-10 Broncos were delivered in 1981, these being ex-US Marine Corps machines. They retained the dark green colouring overall and even the original black serial numbers at the top of the fins.

Following the non-delivery of some Hughes 500 helicopters, the RMorAF accepted a batch of 24 SA.342L Gazelles, half armed with HOT missiles for the anti-armour role and others fitted with GIAT 20mm cannon and rocket pods for anti-guerrilla operations. These machines have a sand and stone camouflage and have a two-letter code on the tail boom. The Italian-built CH-47C Chinook fleet numbers 12 machines: these have a similar finish but incorporate a five-letter code located at the top of the fin.

A common facet of Moroccan markings is the use of both civil registrations and military serials on many RMorAF types, fighters being the exception. However, the presentation of these markings seems to vary between aircraft. Sometimes it is presented as CN-ASG which is a Puma helicopter, on other occasions as CNA-OR, which has been applied to a C-130H Hercules. All the current registrations fall within the CN-AAA to -AZZ block. The discrepancy in style probably indicates different markings information being provided to the various manufacturers by the RMorAF at the time the aircraft were ordered.

Mozambique

The Forca Popular Aerea de Libertacao de Moçambique operates two squadrons of MiG-17F Frescos from Maputo, but reports of MiG-23 Floggers and MiG-21 Fishbeds cannot be confirmed, although some of the latter, flown by East Germans and Cubans, operated for a time against Renamo guerrillas. Markings are carried on wings and fuselage and aircraft are identified by two- or three-digit serial numbers, usually applied on the nose. The national insignia comprises a gun and a hoe within a gearwheel symbolizing the political movement which heralded independence.

Netherlands

The Royal Netherlands Air Force forms part of NATO's 2nd Allied Tactical Air Force and as such plays a vital role in the defence of Western Europe. Known in Dutch as Koninklijke Luchtmacht, the RNethAF has a Tactical Air Command which controls all combat units, equipped almost entirely with General Dynamics F-16A/Bs, the majority of the 213 ordered having been delivered by early 1992. The first F-16 unit was No 322 Squadron, which became operational in May 1981, while the last, No 316 Squadron, received F-16s during 1991. Ten Dutch F-16s are also based in Tucson, Arizona for fighter conversion training.

The national identity marking appears on both sides of the fuselage, above the port wing and below the starboard wing. Unit badges are often applied to both sides of the fin with the individual aircraft number carried below. Three- or four-digit numbers are applied and usually reflect the aircraft construction number. The RNethAF also uses a prefixing system with a single letter allocated to a specific aircraft type. The current list is: A Alouette III (Army); B MBB Bo 105 (Army); C F.27 Troopship/Friendship; H Alouette III (Air Force); J F-16.

The current RNethAF front-line organization is based on a number of squadrons, each with a distinctive badge for which the table below provide· a quick check list.

The great majority of rescue and maintenance markings applied to Dutch combat aircraft are in English, but a limited number are stencilled on the airframe in Dutch, principally emergency instructions around the cockpit area. The standard finish of the F-16 force is two-tone grey as on by US Fighting Falcons. This low-vis finish is accompanied by a sig-

Royal Netherlands Air Force squadron badges

306 Sqn	Eagle's head on black/blue circle	F-16A/B
311 Sqn	Black/white eagle on blue circle	F-16A/B
312 Sqn	Crossed swords and red lightning flash in black circle	F-16A/B
313 Sqn	Eagle on white runway in blue circle	F-16A/B
314 Sqn	Golden centaur in red circle	F-16A/B
315 Sqn	Yellow lion's head in blue circle	F-16A/B
316 Sqn	Brown hawk on yellow disc	F-16A/B
322 Sqn	Red-tailed parrot in white circle	F-16A/B
323 Sqn	Amazon archer in black circle	F-16A/B

nificant reduction in the size of some of the markings and the elimination of some of the bright colours on the fin badges.

The air arm of the Royal Netherlands Navy, the Marine Luchtvaart Dienst, operates Westland Lynx helicopters designated UH-14 or SH-14 depending on the SAR or ASW role, and Lockheed P-3C Orions. Aircraft are allocated three-digit numbers in blocks, the Lynx running from 260 to 283, and the Orions from 300 to 312. KON. MARINE is applied to the rear fuselage of the Orions and the number is carried under the port wing as well as on the fuselage. A base code letter is painted on the fin and standard national markings are carried on fuselage and wings.

Below: RNethAF F-16As of 322 Sqn with two aircraft of 323 Sqn (5th and 6th from camera) flying in echelon formation. Until a few years ago most pilots wore white 'bone-domes', but these could be spotted at considerable distances, compromising the toned-down airframe colours and markings, so dark green has become the standard colour for this type of headwear.

New Zealand

The Royal New Zealand Air Force is an integral part of the country's tri-service defence organization and operates a modest combat element of McDonnell Douglas A-4 Skyhawks, supplemented by 14 BAe Strikemaster 88s, which are currently being phased out in favour of Aermacchi MB.339Cs, 18 of which are on order. There are 21 A-4s in service, single and two-seaters, of which ten are ex-Australian Navy A-4G/TA-4G versions. These and the original RNZAF A-4K/TA-4Ks have been updated and modernised.

These aircraft have had radar fitted, their avionics extensively upgraded, and are equipped to use the AGM-65 Maverick air-to-surface missile. The A-4s are painted in a dark green, mid-tan and olive drab

Nicaragua

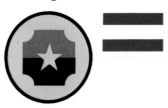

Prior to the civil war in June 1979, the country's air arm was known as the Fuerza Aérea de Nicaragua, but the establishment of a government by the Sandinista National Liberation Front resulted in a renaming to Fuerza Aérea Sandinista. This title is carried in black on the tail booms of all the Soviet-supplied Mil Mi-8 'Hip' and Mil Mi-25 'Hind' attack helicopters as well as the surviving CASA Aviocar transports. Although about 70 Nicaraguan pilots have converted to the MiG-21 in Cuba, this type has signally failed to enter service. The attack mission is flown by a handful of Czech L-39Z Albatrosses supplied by Libya, while six SF-260W Warriors are tasked for COIN operations, supplemented by four Lockheed AT-33s and an equal number of Summit-converted armed O-2-337s, both of which types are of doubtful serviceability. Three-digit serials are the standard form of identifying FAS aircraft, examples being 340 in black on the nose of an Mi-25 and 281 on the nose of an Mi-8. The red, yellow and black national insignia is now carried on all Nicaraguan military aircraft.

Nigeria

Air Force

Navy

Norway

In a similar manner to some other NATO countries, Norway opted for the GD F-16 to meet her present and future military requirements and, today, four of her five front-line combat squadrons are equipped with 60 of these capable fighters. In its present form, the Royal Norwegian Air

camouflage scheme and supposedly give an attack capability 'close to that of an F-16'.

The colours of the New Zealand national marking reflect British influence and the tail flash is identical to that used on some RAF aircraft. The kiwi in the roundel is applied facing forward on both sides of the fuselage, while the wing marking follows US practice and is on the top of the port wing and on the underside of the starboard.

RNZAF aircraft are identified by four-digit numbers prefixed NZ, the A-4s running in a block from NZ6201 with the trainers (TA-4s) from NZ6251, all letters and numbers being in white. The Strikemasters, of which 16 were purchased, have serials from NZ6361 to 6376. To aid identification on the ground, the Skyhawks have the last three numbers repeated in white on the nose. Unit badges of the two squadrons — black and white chequers for 2 Sqn and yellow diamonds for 75 Sqn — are displayed on the engine intakes; the same position applies to the white diamonds forming the 14 Sqn badge on the Strikemasters. Rescue, maintenance and warning stencilling follows standard Western practice.

The Federal Nigerian Air Force uses the national green and white colours for its roundel and fin flash. These colours were adopted in 1959, just before Nigeria's independence from Britain, and represent the country's forests with peace and unity. Backbone of the NAF's combat units are the squadrons flying MiG-21MF fighter-bombers, of which 16 are in service, Jaguars (15) and AlphaJets (22) and 22 L-39 Albatrosses with a further 27 of these on order. All these types are camouflaged, usually in two greens and a light tan scheme on the upper surface and light blue underneath. Each aircraft carries a three-figure identifying serial, prefixed by NAF: the MiGs are in the 650 to 680 range, the Jaguars from 700 and the AlphaJets from 450, and in almost all cases both numbers and letters are in black. An anomaly was the application of the roundel marking on the fins of the MiGs during the mid-1970s. MB.339 trainers of the NAF carry the serial on the top of the port wing together with the roundel. About 20 MBB Bö105s are flown armed with rocket pods.

The Nigerian Navy has recently formed a Fleet Air Arm to operate the three Westland Lynx Mk 89 ASW helicopters delivered in May 1984 for service aboard its only major warship the frigate *Aradu*.

Force, or Kongelige Norske Luftforsvaret, has only existed since 1944 when the Army and Naval Air Services were amalgamated. The RNorAF's delta marking is a postwar design and in line with current NATO practice is being displayed in miniaturized form on the F-16s (and also on the P-3C Orions). Northrop F-5As equip the fifth combat unit and these will remain in service in the fighter lead-in, aggressor, air defence and EW role, and are currently undergoing an avionics update. C-130s, Bell 412 SPs and DHC Twin Otters form the transport force.

Individual aircraft carry a three-digit identification number on the fin which usually represents the last three figures of the aircraft's construction number. Current examples are: F-16A 272-307; F-16B 658-693; P-3B Orion 576, 583, 599-603; C-130H Hercules 952-957; Sea King Mk 43 060, 062, 066, 068-07, 073, 047 and 189.

Squadron badges are sometimes but not invariably applied to the fins of the F-16s and F-5s. The Sea Kings used for SAR duties have REDNINGSTJENESTE along the sides of the cabin, while Coast Guard Lynx helicopters have the legend KYSTVAKT in white on the tail boom.

Oman

Situated on the strategically important Straits of Hormuz — oil gateway to the Arabian Gulf — the Sultanate of Oman has a close affiliation with the Western world and in particular with Great Britain, and with British assistance this moderate Arab country has developed one of the most efficient, if not the largest, air arms in this troubled area.

While future equipment for the combat element of the Sultan of Oman's Air Force (SOAF), or Al Quwwat al Jawwiya al Sultanat Oman, centres on the fleet of BAe Hawk 100/200s ordered in 1990, the present strength consists of 22 Jaguar International attack aircraft. Camouflaged in Dark Earth (BS381C-450) and Light Stone (BS381C-361), these aircraft carry serials between 200 and 224 on the rear fuselage in both figures and Arabic script.

The colour scheme wraps round the whole airframe and the only national insignia is a small blue badge with a crossed swords design in the centre. There have been a number of

Pakistan

Air Force

Navy

The five-pointed star and crescent moon of Islam were adopted by the state of Pakistan in 1947 following independence from Britain and the insignia in a green square forms the fin marking on aircraft of the Pakistan Air Force. The wing and fuselage marking consists of a green and white roundel. Early aircraft were obtained from Britain, but Pakistan gradually moved toward the US sphere of influence, acquiring various types during the 1960s from American manufacturers. Forty three General Dynamics F-16A/Bs are already in the inventory, and another

70 on order, but political considerations make it unlikely that these will be delivered. Two squadrons, Nos 9 and 14, fly F-16s, while Nos 15, 17 and 23 operate Shenyang F-6 Farmers. Three more, Nos 2, 18 and 19, are equipped with Chengdu F-7P Skybolts, and Nos 16 and 26 have A5-III Fantans. A number of Mirage IIIs and 5s remain in service and these are operated by Nos 5 and 8 Squadrons.

Individual aircraft numbers take the form of serials based on the construction number. They are carried on the rear fuselage of most types or on the lower part of the fin as in the case of the F-16s. Three- or four-digit serials are standard, often repeated on the nose, sometimes stencil-split or in the angled US style. Some aircraft retain a natural metal finish, notably the F-6s, while others have varying forms of disruptive camouflage such as the A-5s, which are coloured grey/green/buff over the top surfaces and light grey on the undersurfaces. Other schemes include light grey and dark green (F-6s) and two-tone grey (F-16s).

The PAF applies squadron badges to the fins of its combat aircraft. Examples are 19 Sqn, which has a green cobra on a white circle on its F-6s; 25 Sqn, which has a black eagle different designs and colour combinations for this insignia with some aircraft still carrying the older red and white marking. Apart from the standard rescue and maintenance stencilling, the only other marking is a repeat of the serial number on the nose undercarriage door for ground handling purposes.

Two other front-line types with the SOAF are the Hunter, a batch of 31 having been transferred from Jordan in 1975, and the Strikemaster, which has been operational since 1967. Camouflaged in a new disruptive two-tone grey scheme, these two aircraft conduct ground-attack, patrol and advanced training duties. The Hunters are serialled from 801 onward, while the Strikemasters run from 401 to 424. It seems probable that when the Hawks are delivered, they will also be painted in the two-tone grey scheme.

Other types in service include Short Skyvans and B-N Defenders painted in Dark Green and Dark Earth with white over the cockpit area. Three C-130H Hercules are in use together with some helicopters which are operated on SAR duties along the coastal areas of the country.

A Police Air Wing flies a mixture of types on patrol, surveillance and general transport duties around the Sultanate, and each aircraft carries a civil registration of two letters prefixed A40. Examples are Do 228s received in 1984, A40-CQ and CR. All PAW aircraft carry the organization's crest, usually on the fin.

in a yellow triangle on its F-6s; and 14 Sqn, which has a scimitar in a white circle on its F-6s. The Combat Commanders School has its initials (CCS) on the fins of its F-6s.

In a similar manner to the fighter units, PAF Hercules transports have mostly been camouflaged in green or brown and light stone colours. The title PAKISTAN AIR FORCE is applied prominently above the forward fuselage and by the cockpit windows

Above: These Pakistani A-5 attack aircraft are finished in a feather-edged grey/green/tan camouflage scheme.

is a large single identifying letter, A in the case of C-130B 24141 and S on C-130E 14727, though these letters change as aircraft pass through maintenance. The official squadron badge has been seen applied by the forward entry door on the port side. ▶

The air component of the Pakistan Navy has six Westland Sea King Mk 45s serialled 4510 to 4515 and four Atlantic maritime patrol aircraft with three P-3C Orions on order. The national insignia has an anchor superimposed and a yellow outline.

The Pakistan Army has operated 20 Bell AH-1S Cobras in the anti-tank role for several years now. Other types in use are Puma helicopters from France, Mil Mi-8s from the Soviet Union and home-produced Mushshak (Saab MFI-17) two-seat basic trainers. All carry the title ARMY and the standard national insignia as well as a three- or four-digit serial number.

Paraguay

This land-locked South American country supports three armed services under a unified command. The Fuerza Aérea Paraguaya is mainly a transport and civil aid force with a single combat squadron equipped with the survivors of ten Embraer Xavantes delivered in 1980 as its sole front-line unit. These aircraft carry serials 1001 to 1010 with the last two digits displayed on the nose in black, while national markings are located on wings and fuselage with a small horizontal flash on the fin. Instructional markings on the airframe are in Spanish, including SALMENTO for Rescue and PERIGO for Danger, but the marking signs accord with standard Western practice, including such symbols as red/white ejection seat triangles, 'no step' areas and battery location.

Under the current FAP serialling system numbers are allocated as follows: 0001-0999 trainers and liaison; 1000-1999 jets; 2000-2999 twin-engined transports; 3000-3999 miscellaneous types; 4000-4999 four-engined transports.

Peru

Air Force

Navy

"Look, the flag of liberty!" This exclamation by General Jose de San Martin was prompted by the sight of a large flock of flamingos during this Argentinian patriot's liberation of Peru from the ruling Spanish in 1820. The red and white colours of the birds were adopted for the country's flag, and as a fin flash it is carried by all aircraft operated by the Peruvian Air Force, or Fuerza Aérea Peruana. Roundels are applied in the usual positions on wings and fuselage, but only above the port wing and below the starboard, the opposite locations being reserved for the aircraft serial. Anomalies include Soviet-supplied Sukhoi Su-22 fighter-bombers which carry no fuselage roundels (these and the Antonov An-26s carry a brown and tan camouflage scheme).

Philippines

Bearing a national insignia which closely resembles the American star and bar, the present Philippine Air Force was really only established — with US aid — after World War II. The single fighter squadron, 6th TFS,

When Peru received its first Mirage 5Ps, in 1968, it became the first Latin American country to have Mach 2 aircraft in service. Sixteen, including two two-seat trainers, remain in service, but the spearhead of the force is now the far more potent Mirage 2000, of which 14 are operated. Other combat aircraft in service include various marks of Canberra received from Britain between 1957 and 1978, and about 30 small Cessna A-37B "Tweety Bird" light attack and FAC aircraft.

FAP aircraft serialling takes a familiar form with the following system: 100 fighters; 200 bombers/fighter-bombers; 300 tactical transports; 400 trainers; 500 miscellaneous types; 600 helicopters; 700 communications types.

Above: Peruvian A-37Bs in standard FAP insignia. This light attack jet was developed from the T-37 trainer.

The FAP appears to leave gaps within some serial blocks which can make assessment of Air Force strength difficult. However, this is not the case with every type in service. Grupo (squadron) badges have been noted on some aircraft and most of the transport and helicopters carry the titles FUERZA AEREA DEL PERU along the fuselage or cabin area. Apart from the tactical camouflages used, FAP rescue and training types employ bright red colours for high visibility, some helicopters being almost totally covered in bright fluorescent orange.

operates Northrop F-5A/B Freedom Fighters, and four ex-Taiwanese aircraft were supplied under the US Military Assistance Program in 1989 to keep this unit viable, but this notwithstanding, by late 1990 these aircraft were rarely flown. The F-8H Crusaders of 7th TFS have been phased out due to insurmountable maintenance problems.

All PAF machines carry the legend PHIL AIR FORCE, on the nose in the case of the F-5A/Bs and T/RT-33s, and on the centre fuselage for the others, while national markings are

carried on the fuselage and above the port wing and below the starboard. Individual aircraft are identified by the former USAF/USN serial of which the last three digits are usually applied larger on the fuselage.

Combat activity, generally centreing on COIN against various factions of anti-government guerrillas who infest the remote areas of the islands, is carried out by just two fixed wing types; the Lockheed T-33s of the 105th TFS, and the T-28D Trojans of 16 and 18 Attack Squadrons. The seven survivors of the original batch ▶

of T-33s were supplemented by an equal number of ex-USAF machines in 1988, while about 14 Trojans remain operational out of the original 55. New equipment is desperately needed, but lack of funds precludes its acquisition. The only new aircraft to enter the inventory in recent years were 18 S.211 trainers ordered in 1988 and assembled in the Philippines by PADC. The surviving SF.260s have been relegated to the training role, and some have been deactivated altogether, the unit which formerly operated them, the 17th Attack squadron, now flies Bell AH-1 Cobra gunships in the COIN and close-air support mission.

Philippine Naval Aviation has a force of around 10 Britten-Norman Defenders, and rotary wing assets amount to a similar number of MBB Bo.105s. The Defenders carry PHILIPPINE NAVY along the sides of

the fuselage and the constructor's number in white on the fin. The army also flies a small collection of transport helicopters, including MBB Bo.105s, Hughes 369Ds and Bell

Poland

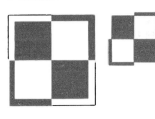

The Wojska Lotnicze i Obrony Powietrznej was formed on the demise of the Warsaw Pact in April 1990 by the amalgamation of the Air Force and Air Defence Force. The second largest air arm in Eastern Europe, the WLiOP operates over 500 combat aircraft of Russian design. The most important type numerically is the MiG-21 Fishbed, with lesser numbers of MiG-23MF Floggers, Su-20/22 Fitters, and a handful of MiG-29 Fulcrums, further orders for which were cancelled in 1989. Interceptors are generally finished in air superiority grey, while attack aircraft normally carry green/brown/dark grey camouflage. All these aircraft carry the red and white national insignia on wings and tail and serialing appears to be in blocks of up to four-digit numbers, sometimes apparently stencilled, and

applied to the forward part of the aircraft. Taking the Su-20 as an example of just how difficult it is to assess the number of any type in Polish service, these aircraft have carried numbers ranging from 03 to 04 through to the 6250 range.

UH-1H Iroquois.
Some Government-operated aircraft have their serial numbers prefixed RP, standing for Republic of Philippines.

Above: One of the SF.260WP Warrior COIN aircraft in service with the Philippine Air Force photographed alongside a similarly tasked T-28D.

Above: Poland built the Soviet Mi-2 Hoplite helicopter, and many of these reconnaissance and liaison machines are still in service. These three are shown in an unusual green/grey/olive drab camouflage colour scheme.

Portugal

The Portuguese Air Force or Forca Aérea Portuguesa uses the Cross of Redemption as the main wing and fuselage marking while the unequal fin flash follows the layout of the national flag with red, representing blood shed, taking more area than the green, meaning hope. The sharp end of the Forca Aérea consists of two Esquadras, Nos 302 and 304, equipped with A-7P Corsair IIs. The former is primarily an anti-shipping outfit, while the latter specialises in-ground attack. Both have to carry responsibility for air defence, pending the arrival of refurbished F-16A/Bs in 1994, which will form a dedicated air defence unit.

Six Lockheed P-3P Orions are used for maritime patrol, while ex-Luftwaffe AlphaJets have been offered in return for basing facilities at Beja. C.212 Aviocars handle a ▶

81

multitude of tasks, including SAR around the Azores, in which they are supplemented by SA.330C Pumas.

Virtually all aircraft carry the green/brown camouflage scheme known as NATO South, although the T-33 fleet, which was phased out during 1991, carried an all-grey finish. Serials of the A-7Ps commenced at 5501 in sequence, and airframe stencilling is in both Portuguese and English. The original five C-130H Hercules were serialled 6801 to 6805. The Portuguese serial system has the first digit indicating type.

Portuguese role numbers

1	Single-engined trainers
2	Twin-engined trainers
3	Liaison aircraft
4	Fighter-bombers
5	Fighters
6	Transports
7	Miscellaneous
8	Staff transports
9	Helicopters

Below: A Portuguese G.91T in the 'NATO South' green and tan camouflage scheme.

Qatar

The Qatar national flag closely resembles that flown by Bahrain, but the serrated line divides white and maroon instead of red. Miniature presentations of the emblem form part of the tail flash carried on Qatar Emiri Air Force aircraft, while the roundel is displayed in the standard positions on wings and fuselage. The first jets used by the air arm were three single-seat Hunters and a two-seat trainer delivered in 1971. These carried the serials QA10 to QA13 and flew mainly coastal patrols against smugglers and air defence sorties around the State. AlphaJets arrived in 1980 for training duties and like the Hunters wore desert camouflage with medium blue undersides and the codes QA50 to QA55.

With many of the surrounding countries now flying much more sophisticated combat aircraft, Qatar decided to invest in a more appropriate defensive force. The result was an order for 12 Mirage F.1EDA fighters and two F.1DDA conversion trainers, their serials being QA71 to QA82 and QA61 and QA62 respectively. Other types in use include Westland Commandos, SA.330J Super Pumas and 16 Gazelles. Qatar Police Helicopters carry the prefix QP.

Romania

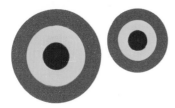

The overthrow of the Ceasusescu regime, coupled with the dissolution of the Warsaw Pact, appears to have had little effect on the Romanian armed forces, which are equipped mainly with Russian or indigenous equipment, and the air arm is no exception: Fortele Aeriene ale Republicii Socialiste Românîa has 12 air defence squadrons equipped with MiG-29A/B Fulcrums, MiG-23MF/UM Floggers and over 100 MiG-21 Fishbeds. The two attack regiments operate IAR-93A/B Oraos, of which about 200 are in service or on order. Markings incorporating the national colours of blue, yellow and red are applied to the wings and tail of the MiGs, the nose being reserved for the individual aircraft number. Examples are 709, 710, 712, 713 and 714 in black on natural metal finish MiG-21s, 32 and 35 in white on camouflaged Pumas (which are built under licence in Romania by ICA and designated IAR-330), and 706 and 716 on Mil Mi-8 helicopters.

El Salvador

Heavily supported by the United States, the right-wing government in El Salvador continues its guerrilla war against left-wing factions. Usurprisingly, the combat element of the Fuerza Aerea Salvadorena consists mainly of counter-insurgency aircraft. Seven worn-out ex-Israeli Ouragans are on strength, although whether they have any useful life remaining is debatable. The truly operational aircraft are 10 A-37B Dragonflies, four CM.170 Magisters, a handful of 0-2A Super Skymasters and seven AC-47 gunships, supplemented by a dozen Rallye 235GS Guerriers. Bell UH-1H/M Hueys are the most numerous rotary wing type. Most FAS aircraft carry the national marking in the standard positions with the blue/white/blue flash applied horizontally across the rudder.

The serialling of FAS aircraft appears to follow no logical pattern, some aircraft having a two-digit number while others have three, apparently unrelated to the original construction number of the type. Some examples are the IAI Arava light transports which are 801, 802, and so on, the Ouragans running from 700 to 717 and Cessna T-41s which are 90, 91, etc. Serials are prefixed FAS and some transports, such as the Douglas C-118 301, carry the air force title in large capital letters along the top of the fuselage.

Saudi Arabia

The main feature of the Saudi Arabian national flag is a religious inscription in white on a green field which, translated, means 'There is no God but Allah, and Muhammad is the Prophet of Allah'. Green is the traditional colour of the Fatimid dynasty of Arabia established by Muhammad's daughter Fatima, chosen because ▶

Muhammad reputedly wore a green turban. On aircraft of the Royal Saudi Air Force, or Al Quwwat al Jawwiya al Sa'udiya, a representation of the flag is displayed on each side of the fin (read from right to left). The official title of the air arm is applied in green on almost all equipment and repeated in Arabic immediately above. Serials, too, are marked in both styles.

Air defence is the task of 80 F-15C/D Eagles in Nos 5, 6, 13 and 42 Squadrons, in which they are supplemented by 24 Panavia Tornado F.3s in Nos 29 and 34 Squadrons. Air defence aircraft are painted a uniform light grey.

The interdiction mission is flown by Nos 7 and 66 Squadrons, equipped with the Tornado IDS, while F-5E/F squadrons Nos 3, 10 and 17, provide close air support. Both types carry a disruptive sand/stone/green camouflage scheme with standard markings. Two early Tornados were numbered 701 and 704, while the F-5Es carry a follow-on to their USAF serial; for example 00918 was once 73-18.

Badges are a feature of some RSAF aircraft, notably the transports of 4 Sqn at Jeddah, which have a full unit badge by the port-side front

Right: This view shows serial number 701, the first Tornado IDS delivered to Saudi Arabia. Painted in a disruptive pattern camouflage of sand, stone and green, it carries the green national markings on the tail fin and roundels on the front fuselage, port upper and starboard lower wings. ROYAL SAUDI AIR FORCE and the Arabic equivalent are written on the front fuselage.

Singapore

Republic of Singapore Air Force has changed its insignia twice since its inception in 1965. Commencing with a conventional red/white roundel, it later switched to a red/white finned yin-yang design. It is now reportedly changing to a stylised lion's head inside a circle. The marking is carried on the fuselage and wings of the F-16A/B Fighting Falcons, F-5E Tiger IIs and A-4S Skyhawks which make up the combat element of the force.

The F-16A/Bs carry a two tone grey finish with a coloured unit stripe at the top of the fin, while the F-5Es currently wear both two tone grey and light and medium green/sand finishes, even within the same unit. The F-5s carry serials in the 800 range, applied on the fin and nose, while the Skyhawks, sprayed in green and tan camouflage for the low-level attack role, have numbers in the 600 range applied on the rear fuselage in white with the last two digits displayed on the nose. An example of the latter is No 647, which has 47 on the nose, a Phoenix badge under the cockpit window signifying No 143 'Phoenix' Sqn, and a yellow and black rudder. Other units also have names such as 140 'Osprey', 141 'Merlin', 142 'Gryphon', 120 'Condor' and 130 'Eagle'.

Skyhawks re-engined with the General Electric F404 appear however to carry serials in the 900 range, i.e. A-4S 923.

fuselage entrance door, and 5 Sqn, whose Eagles have a small unit marking on the fin. Instructional and rescue markings over the airframe are often applied in both English and Arabic, the first aid marking taking the form of the Muslim crescent in the place of the red cross.

Hercules transports operated by the air arm carry the full title of the force along the forward fuselage, small representations of the national insignia on fuselage and wings and the three-digit serial on the fin in black, for example 725 and 732, the 25 and 32 being repeated on the nose. In addition to the serials noted above, other types are SF.260MS 120, 121, etc; SF.260W 151, 152, etc; SIAI-Marchetti S.211 380, 381, etc; and HS Hunter 500, 501, etc.

Below: A TA-4S of the Singapore Air Force, with the national marking on the fuselage rear.

Somalia

The national markings of Somalia date from 1954 and the adoption of the white star originally used by the southern part of the country; the Somali Air Force (Dayuuradaha Xoogga Dalka Somaliyeed) took the insignia and formed a roundel which is currently used on wings and fuselage. A handful of MiG-17As, -21s and Shenyang F-6s remain on strength (most of which are unserviceable) but more recently Somalia has turned to the West, and in particular to Italy, for both economic and military aid. The result was the delivery of some SF.260W armed trainers (serialled 60-SBC, -SBD etc), two G.222 transports (AM94- AM97) and some HS Hunters acquired from Kenya and Abu Dhabi. Three ex-Abu Dhabi Islanders are also in use. A leaping tiger in yellow was applied to the nose of the G.222s.

South Africa

Since 1957 aircraft of the South African Air Force have carried the national marking shown above, consisting of a plan of the fort at Cape Town enclosing the springbok symbol. It is located in the standard positions on most aircraft although for service in the 'operational area' it is sometimes deleted from the more prominent positions. The tail stripes represent the national flag and originate from the emblem of the Dutch Prince of Orange, which was brought to the country by the early settlers in the seventeenth century. It is sometimes sprayed over the whole rudder, as on the Mirage F.1s, or as a much smaller oblong on the fins, as on the Harvards still in service. Transports which carry camouflage do not generally use a fin flash.

Government and VIP aircraft such as the BAe.125s display the legend S.A. AIR FORCE.

From 1975 to 1989, the South African Air Force was heavily committed to the war in Angola, which involved almost every tactical aircraft type in the inventory at one time or another. Both MiG-21 Fishbeds and MiG-23 Floggers of the Angolan Air Force have fallen to the guns and missiles of South African fighters, but the introduction of beyond visual range missiles by the latter caused a reduction in air activity towards the end of the war. Helicopters were the workhorses of the war with Alouette IIIs and Pumas the most widely used.

Of the main combat types in SAAF use, the Mirage F.1CZ fighter and F.1AZ attack version are the most important. The serials applied on the rear fuselage run from 200 to 215 on the former type and 216 to 247 on the latter. Camouflage for the attack version is Olive Drab (BS381C-298) and Deep Buff (360) with Light Admiralty Grey (697) underneath, but the interceptor Mirage F.1CZs wear and all over light grey finish for the air superiority role.

Many Mirage IIIs of different types, fighters, trainers and reconnaissance aircraft, were once in the inventory, serialled from 800 to 857. Twenty nine of these have been singled out for conversion to Cheetah standard, while the remainder were retired during 1991. The Cheetah is a rebuilt Mirage III with canard foreplanes and a modern avionics suite. It is very similar to the Israeli Kfir C-7 in appearance, but retains the French Atar engine instead of having GE J79s fitted. Other types retired during 1990/91 were the Buccaneer, Canberra, Piaggio P.166, and Super Frelon and Wasp helicopters. The Italian-designed single-seat MB.326KC Impala II was built by Atlas Aircraft in South Africa. About 120 two seater Atlas Impala Is are currently in service, numbered between 460-610, plus nearly 80 single seater Impala II light attack aircraft with serials between 1001 and 1090. Like most tactical aircraft, they have the last two digits repeated on the nose in black and their camouflage is a disruptive scheme of Olive Drab (298), Dark Earth (450) and Light Admiralty Grey (697).

Fixed-wing transport includes 7 C-130B Hercules, 9 Transalls about 10 C-47 Dakotas, 6 C-54 Skymasters and a few BAe 125s for communications duties.

Squadron badges reflect long traditions in the SAAF and are carried by a number of types, usually on the fin but sometimes on the engine intake

SAAF squadrons, badges and aircraft

1 Sqn	RAF eagle holding a Crusader's shield	Mirage F.1AZ
2 Sqn	Flying cheetah with motto 'Upward and onward'	Cheetah
3 Sqn	Hornet with motto 'Always fighting'	Mirage F.1CZ
4 Sqn	Bat on blue circle with motto 'Death to the enemy'	Impala II

or under the cockpit. Current examples are as shown.

The helicopter force of Alouette IIIs and SA.330 Pumas has a uniform colour scheme consisting of Olive Drab and Dark Earth with two or three digits identifying the individual aircraft. The serial numbers of the Alouettes range from 23 to 637 and those of the Pumas from 120 to 186.

Soviet Union (CIS)

In the late 1980s, the Soviet Union as it then was, possessed a massive fleet of nearly 15,000 aircraft in five separate commands. Long Range Aviation operated about 750 bombers, of which the Tupolev Tu-160 Blackjack was the most modern. About 20 Blackjacks are in service, but production is reported to have been halted in 1991. The only other aircraft with the range to be termed strategic are the 147 turbo-prop powered Tu-95/142 Bear series. Two hundred or so relatively modern Tu-22M Backfires can be considered theatre strategic, while the remainder consists of elderly Tu-22 Blinders and even older Tu-16 Badgers.

Frontal Aviation, covering interdiction, strike, close air support, tactical reconnaissance and air superiority over the battlefield, had nearly 10,000 aircraft, including almost 4,000 helicopters. Frontal Aviation consisted of 16 air armies totalling roughly 100 regiments, plus a handful of autonomous squadrons. Each air army was assigned to a Military ▶

Below: A close-up of the cockpit of 'red 99', a Soviet MiG-23.

District. The main types in FA service were MiG-23 Flogger B, MiG-27 Flogger D, MiG-29 Fulcrum A, Su-17 Fitter C/D/H, Su-24 Fencer, and Su-25 Frogfoot. The bulk of the rotary wing force consisted of Mi-8/17 Hip and Mi-24 Hind.

The role of the Air Defence Force (PVO) is self-explanatory. It had about 1,250 interceptors, comprising Su-27 Flanker B, rapidly replacing Su-15/21 Flagons; MiG-23 Flogger B/G, MiG-25 Foxbat E, and MiG-31 Foxhound. It was backed by Il-76 Mainstay AWACS aircraft, replacing Tu-126 Moss.

Military Transport Aviation ranged from the single engined An-2 Colt biplane to the massive Antonov An-124 Condor, with the most numerous type being the Il-76 Candid.

Naval Aviation was mainly land based, with Backfires as the spearhead, Bears for long range MR and anti-shipping missions, and Su-17 Fitters for short range attack. The carrier component consisted of Yak-38 Forgers and ASW helicopters, but Flankers and Fulcrums were to join them when the first real Russian carrier became operational.

This was more or less the position prior to events in the early 'nineties. The first of which was the demand for independence by the three Baltic states, Estonia, Lithuania and Latvia. This was followed by the formal

NATO reporting names

Backfire	Tupolev Tu-22M
Badger	Tupolev Tu-16
Beagle	Ilyushin Il-28
Bear	Tupolev Tu-95/142
Bison	Myasischev M-4
Blackjack	Tupolev Tu-160
Blinder	Tupolev Tu-22
Brewer	Yakovlev Yak-28
Fagot	Mikoyan MiG-15
Farmer	Mikoyan MiG-19
Fencer	Sukhoi Su-24
Fiddler	Tupolev Tu-28
Firebar	Yakovlev Yak-28P
Fishbed	Mikoyan MiG-21
Fitter	Sukhoi Su-7/-17/-20/-22
Flagon	Sukhoi Su-15
Flanker	Sukhoi Su-27
Flogger	Mikoyan MiG-23/-27
Forger	Yakovlev Yak-36
Foxbat	Mikoyan MiG-25
Foxhound	Mikoyan MiG-31
Freestyle	Yakovlev Yak-141
Fresco	Mikoyan MiG-17
Frogfoot	Sukhoi Su-25
Fulcrum	Mikoyan MiG-29
Camber	Ilyushin Il-86
Camp	Antonov An-8
Candid	Ilyushin Il-76
Careless	Tupolev Tu-154
Cash	Antonov An-28
Clank	Antonov An-30
Classic	Ilyushin Il-62
Cleat	Tupolev Tu-114
Cline	Antonov An-32
Clobber	Yakovlev Yak-42
Clod	Antonov An-14
Coaler	Antonov An-72/74
Cock	Antonov An-22
Codling	Yakovlev Yak-40

Coke	Antonov An-24
Colt	Antonov An-2
Condor	Antonov An-124
Cookpot	Tupolev Tu-124
Coot	Ilyushin Il-18
Coot-A	Ilyushin Il-20
Cossack	Antonov An-225
Crate	Ilyushin Il-14
Creek	Yakovlev Yak-12
Crusty	Tupolev Tu-134
Cub	Antonov An-12
Curl	Antonov An-26
Halo	Mil Mi-26
Harke	Mil Mi-10
Havoc	Mil Mi-28
Haze	Mil Mi-14
Helix	Kamov Ka-27/-32
Hermit	Mil Mi-34
Hind	Mil Mi-24/-25
Hip	Mil Mi-8
Hokum	Kamov Ka-34
Hoodlum	Kamov Ka-26
Hook	Mil Mi-6
Hoplite	Mil Mi-2
Hormone	Kamov Ka-25
Hound	Mil Mi-4
Madcap	Antonov An-72 AEW
Maestro	Yakovlev Yak-28U
Mail	Beriev Be-12
Mainstay	Illyushin Il-76 AWACS
Max	Yakovlev Yak-18
May	Ilyushin Il-38
Maya	LET L-29 Delfin
Midas	Ilyushin Il-78
Midget	Mikoyan MiG-15UTI
Mongol	Mikoyan MiG-21U/UM
Moose	Yakovlev Yak-11
Moss	Tupolev Tu-126
Moujik	Sukhoi Su-7U
Mystic	Myasischev M-17

Above: This 'Bear-H' has a natural metal finish and wears only basic national insignia.

renaming of the Soviet Union as the Union of Sovereign States. Then when the Ukraine definitely, and some other states possibly, also decided to secede, it became the Commonwealth of Independent States (CIS) in 1991.

At the time of writing, early in 1992, everything seems in a state of flux. The first proposal was to keep the existing homogenous setup as a mutual protection package under the aegis of CIS, but this is no longer likely. The Ukraine has announced its intention to have its own armed forces; the Baltic states will almost certainly follow suit, as may other independent minded republics such as Byelorussia. This will probably give rise to a plethora of new aircraft markings over the next few years. For example, it is strongly rumoured that the Ukraine will adopt a roundel in the national colours, yellow and blue, while it seems possible that the Baltic states will revert to the colours worn in the 1930s. It is also probable that the CIS will adopt new national markings based on the red, white and pale blue of the Russian national flag. But for the moment, the old USSR markings still apply.

Currently all combat aircraft carry red stars, usually outlined in white or yellow, on wings, fuselage and fins.

During the forty years of the Cold War, the true designation of Russian aircraft was often not known to the West until years after service entry. They were therefore given reporting names by the Air Standards Co-ordinating Committee of NATO,

following the standard code of B for bombers, C for Cargo aircraft, F for fighters, H for helicopters, and M for trainers and miscellaneous. As new variants of existing types were identified, they were given suffix letters to differentiate them. Anomalies in this area are MiG-23/27s, all of which are called Flogger, and Su-7/17/20/22s, all of which are Fitters.

Strategic bombers carry hardly any markings apart from the national insignia, and these tend to be carried on wings and fin only. This was the case with Blackjack when it appeared at Tuschino in August 1989 in an all-white finish. Various Backfires, finished in mid-grey topside and light grey underneath are the same, but often have a two digit serial near the top of the fin. This also applies to most Bears.

Fighters carry large 'bort' numbers in red, yellow or blue, usually on the nose. The shape of Fulcrum has led to difficulties however, and some examples have the number on the intake sides beneath the wing, while in a departure from tradition, some have been seen with large numerals on the fins.

Early air superiority fighters and interceptors usually had a bare metal finish, but this gave way to all-over light grey, while Fulcrum and Flanker wear a two tone blue/grey air superiority finish. Squadron or regimental badges have traditional- ▶

Above: A line-up of Su-17s show their two-digit 'bort' numbers in blue with a white outline.

ly never been carried, but unit efficiency award markings, typically a stylised aircraft superimposed on a red pentagon, have been seen.

Attack aircraft and battlefield helicopters are camouflaged. This varies considerably in style and colour; two greens and brown, brown, sand and green, and virtually any permutation from these have all been seen at different times. Fixed wing aircraft normally have pale undersides, but helicopters have a wrap-around scheme. An anomaly here is the Su-24, which is seen in both grey and camouflaged finishes.

Ship-borne Naval Air Force machines can be identified by the naval ensign, although this is not carried by land-based types. Carrier machines are finished in dark blue/grey all over. Typically Yak-38 Forgers, operating from Kiev-class carriers, show two digit numbers in yellow on the forward fuselage just astern of the naval ensign.

Below: This MiG-23 'Flogger-G' fighter is painted in camouflage more suited to attack aircraft.

Spain

One of NATO's southern members, Spain received its 72nd and final McDonnell Douglas EF-18A/B Hornet in 1990, and the type is now well established in service. These aircraft, like their predecessors over the past 50 years, carry the red and yellow roundel of Aragon, colours which date back to the twelfth century, when they were used by the Kingdom of Aragon. The rudder marking of a black diagonal cross on a white background is more recent and only dates from the Spanish Civil War of the late 1930s. The Spanish Air Force, or Ejército del Aire, has a combat force of some 200 aircraft operating under the auspices of three of the four main commands, Air Combat, Tactical Air and Air Com-

mand of the Canaries; the fourth is Air Transport. Other types in service include 23 Mirage IIIEE/DEs, 60 Mirage F.1CE/EE/BEs, nine RF-4C Phantom IIs, and 48 CASA-built F-5A/B/RF-5As. Spain is a participant in the EFA programme, and is updating the Mirage IIIs and F-5s to extend their operational lives until it enters service. Spanish military aircraft carry individual serial numbers, prefixed by an aircraft code which is allocated to each aircraft type.

Spanish role prefixes

A	Attack
C	Fighter
D	Diverse
E	Trainer
H	Helicopter
P	Patrol
R	Reconnaissance
T	Transport
TK	Transport-tanker
VA	V/STOL attack

An example of the system is a Mirage F1CE which has C14-18 applied in black on its wing, individually the 18th aircraft of the 14th type (the Mirage F-1). Where aircraft have a dual role or a specialized task a combination of letters is carried, such as CR12 for the reconnaissance version of the Phantom. Aircraft operating in the Spanish Air Force, ▶

Below: Spain acquired 40 F-4C Phantoms, this being the 23rd; it has the markings of 121 Escuadron on the engine intake. National insignia is small and colours are Vietnam style.

Army and Navy carry the basic letter/number designators shown.

Spanish type designations

A9	S F - 5 A
AE9	S F - 5 B
AR9	S R F - 5 A
C11	Mirage IIIEE
CE11	Mirage IIIDE
CR12	RF-4C Phantom
C14	Mirage F.1CE
CE14	Mirage F.1BE
C15	EF-18A Hornet
CE15	EF-18B Hornet
D2	F.27-400MPA Maritime
E18	Piper Navajo
E19	Piper Aztec
E20	Beech Baron
E24	Beech Bonanza
E25	CASA 101 Aviojet
E26	ENAER T.35 Pillan
HE7	Bell 47G Sioux
HU8	Bell UH-1B/204
HS9	SH-3D/G Sea King
HU10	Bell UH-1H
HR12	Bell OH-58A/206
HS13	Hughes 500M
HA14	Bell AH-1G Cobra
HA/HE/HR/HU15	MBB Bö 105C
HD16	Alouette III
HT17	CH-47 Chinook
HS/HU18	Agusta-Bell AB-212ASW
HT19	SA.330 Puma
HE20	Hughes 269
HD/HT21	AS.332 Super Puma
HU22	MBB BK117
P3	P-3A/B Orion
T9	DHC-4 Caribou
T10	C-130H Hercules
TK10	KC-130H Hercules
T11	Falcon 20
T/TE/TR12	CASA 212 Aviocar
T15	DC-8
T16	Falcon 50
T17	Boeing 707
T18	Falcon 900
T19	Airtech CN.235
U9	Dornier Do 27
UD13	Canadair CL-215
VA1	AV-8A Matador
VAE1	TAV-8A Matador
VA2	AV-8B Matador II

Right: A Spanish Navy AV-8A displaying naval markings on the fin and fuselage.

In addition to this system, Spanish aircraft also have a unit coding which indicates the Ala (Wing) and the individual machine. The first two numerals indicate the Wing, while the second two are assigned according to standard block codes based on type/function. This has led to some confusion among spotters as aircraft were renumbered. For example, EF-18B Hornet serialled CE15-6 (sixth aircraft of type CE15) of Ala 15 (an unfortunate coincidence of type and unit) carried 15-06 on the nose at first, but now bears 15-75. Up to four squadrons make up an Ala, though the normal complement is two, and each squadron wears the wing badge, the main ones being listed below:

Fighter wing 11 (two squadrons of Mirage IIIs):. Three diving birds in blue on a white disc.

Fighter wing 12 (two squadrons of

Hornets and one of reconnaissance Phantoms): Dark blue wildcat's head. Fighter wing 14 (two squadrons of Mirage F.1s): Don Quixote with three Mirages and No 14 in red.
Attack wing 21 (one squadron of SF-5s): Blue and white shield with black F-5 silhouette.
Wing 46, in the Canaries (one squadron of Mirage F.1s and one of Aviocars): Black 46 on red circle.

Naval aircraft

Spanish Naval aircraft bear the legend MARINA on the rear fuselage of the AV-8 Matadors and on the tail boom of the helicopters. Wing markings for the Matadors consist of standard roundels in addition to the individual aircraft number and unit on the upper surface of the port wing and the word MARINA with roundel above the starboard side. A winged anchor symbol is also carried.

Sri Lanka

Independent from Britain since 1948, Sri Lanka was formerly named Ceylon and its air arm, the Sri Lanka Air Force, has an insignia formed from the main elements of the national flag. The green and orange in the bars represent the Muslims and Hindu Tamils respectively, while the maroon and yellow are the colours of the old flag of Kandy, the ancient kingdom in the centre of the island. Transport and liaison duties are the main tasks of this small force which has a collection of helicopters and fixed-wing types for both civil and military use although COIN missions against Tamil guerrillas are flown by SF.260TPs and Bell 206 and 212 helicopters fitted out with machine guns and rockets.

Serials consist of a prefix letter C for Ceylon and a role letter: A for advanced trainers, C single-engined transports, F fighters, H helicopters, J jet aircraft, R multi-engined transports, S surveillance aircraft and T trainers. Thus CH-531 and -532 are SA.365C Dauphins; CC-650 and -651 are Cessna 337s; CR-841 is a Super King Air; and CR-801 and -802 are DH Herons.

Sweden

The Kingdom of Sweden has remained determinedly neutral over the past four decades although bounded by NATO on one side and the now defunct Warsaw Pact on the other. ▶

Her borders are with Norway in the west, fellow neutral Finland in the north and, across the sea, the Baltic republics, Poland and Russia. To reduce the reliance on outside arms suppliers, Sweden has developed an industrial base which has designed and produced the past and present military equipment of all three services and is currently working on the country's future needs to continue doing so into the twenty-first century. The Royal Swedish Air Force (Flygvapnet) has an interceptor force of some 200 aircraft consisting of new JA 37 Viggens and older J 35 Drakens, both products of Saab. From 1993, the Air Force will receive a planned 140 JAS 39 Gripen to replace the Viggen fleet, variants of which are also in use in the attack and reconnaissance roles.

The Swedish national marking bears the colours of the flag but incorporates the three crowns derived from the ancient state coat-of-arms dating from 1364. The insignia is carried on the forward fuselage and wings of all Sweden's combat aircraft. Two other prominent markings are located on each aircraft: on the nose is the number of the Flottilj (wing) to which the aircraft belongs, and on the tail is a two-digit number allocated sequentially through the two combat squadrons which currently form a wing.

On the attack and reconnaissance Viggens, the tail code is applied in dayglo orange over the complicated splinter camouflage pattern adopted in the 1970s. This consists of black green, mid-green, light green and stone with light grey on the under-surfaces. Fighter versions of this capable canard design have recently acquired a light grey low-visibility finish in accord with other air forces in Europe. Serial numbers on the combat types are applied in 3in (76mm) figures on the rear fuselage, in yellow on camouflage and black on natural metal finishes, and consist of five digits, those on the Viggens running from 37000.

Military aircraft in Sweden are given different designations from those operated by other countries. Each type has a role prefix letter followed by a sequential number. While the number remains the same, an aircraft having a change of role will also have a change of prefix. The current list is: A Anfallplan (attack); Hkp Helikopter: J Jaktplan (fighter); S Spanplan (reconnaissance); Sk Skolplan (trainer); Tp Transportplan. Swedish military aircraft and their designations are as shown.

RSAF aircraft designations

Hkp 2	Alouette II
Hkp 3	Agusta-Bell AB.204B
Hkp 4	Vertol 107-II
Hkp 5	Hughes 300
Hkp 6	Agusta-Bell AB.206A
J 32	Saab Lansen
J 35/SK 35	
	Saab Draken
JA/AJ/SF/SK/SH 37	
	Saab Viggen
JAS 39	Gripen
Sk 50	Saab 91 Safir
Sk 60	Saab 105
Sk 61	Scottish Aviation Bulldog
Tp 84	Lockheed C-130 Hercules
Tp 85	Caravelle III
Tp 86	Rockwell Sabreliner
Tp 88	Swearingen Metro

The Viggen has been produced in five different versions: the AJ 37 attack aircraft, JA 37 fighter, SF 37 reconnaissance, Sk 37 trainer and SH 37 maritime surveillance aircraft.

Stencilling and maintenance instructions are applied in Swedish, ▶

Above: Without doubt one of the most complex camouflage schemes ever applied to a production aircraft, this four-colour pattern has been applied to Swedish Viggens since the early 1970s. This AJ 37 attack version carries the nose code of F13 Wing and, coincidentally, the individual aircraft number 13 on the fin below the unit badge.

Left: In plan, the prominent wing insignia contrast strongly against the Viggen's disruptive colour scheme. An impending attack on Sweden would prompt the dispersal of the Flygvapnet fleet to prearranged locations on the country's road system where prepositioned fuel and ammunition would sustain it.

the most obvious being FARA (Danger) painted on the engine intakes. Also note that the fin code number is repeated in black on the Viggens' main undercarriage doors. For tactical exercises, Drakens have large white numbers applied to their wings, the overall proportions being 250cm (98½ in) in height and 120cm (47¼ in) in width.

Above: The angled undernose indicates a photoreconnaissance S 35E Dracken. Few of these remain in RSAF service, their role being taken over by the SH/SF 37 Viggen: F16 at Angelholm and F15 at Uppsala are now the only Draken Wings and only the former is likely to retain the type.

Switzerland

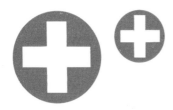

A feature of Switzerland's neutrality is the country's preparedness for war. Stretches of roadway are specially designated as runways, mountains have huge caverns buried in them to accommodate whole squadrons of aircraft and their supplies, and almost all Swiss citizens are members of either the full-time military or the part-time militia. The Swiss Air Force, or Flugwaffe, is a branch of the Army and its first role is to detect, identify and react to foreign air incursions from any direc-

tion, while its second task is to support the ground troops and provide them with a protective air umbrella. The three types of combat aircraft in service, totalling some 260 aircraft, are Hawker Hunters, Northrop F-5Es and Dassault-Breguet Mirage IIIs. The main insignia is identical to that on the Swiss flag and is applied in the standard wing positions and on the fin on all military aircraft. The fuselage is reserved in most cases for the identification number, of four digits in the case of the front-line machines and of three on support types.

Using a style similar to that employed by other air arms, the Swiss serialling prefix system has an identifying role letter: A for Anfänger (learner, or trainer); C Utility; J Jägd (hunter, or fighter); R Reconnaissance; U Übungsflugzeug (practice aircraft, or trainer); V Verbindungs

(communications). The Swiss are in the throes of acquiring their next fighter, and bitter arguments rage in the Government about the cost of such a purchase. The McDonnell-Douglas F/A-18 Hornet has been chosen over the Mirage 2000 and MiG-29, although in 1992 the final decision on expenditure was deferred for at least a year.

Above: J-3202, one of the 12 Northrop F-5F trainers delivered to the Swiss Air Force.

One of the important duties of the Flugwaffe is SAR operations in mountains that cover much of the country. Helicopters designated for such tasks include French Alouette II and Alouette III machines. ▶

Swiss Air Force serial numbers

Pilatus P-3	A-801 to A-873
Pilatus PC-7	A-902 to A-941
Dassault-Breguet Mirage IIIS	J-2301 to J-2336
Northrop F-5E/F	J-3001 to J-3207 +
Hawker Hunter F.58/T.68	J-4001 to J-4208
Dassault-Breguet Mirage IIIRS	R-2101 to R-2118
Dassault-Breguet Mirage IIIBS	U-2001 range
Sud Alouette III	V-201 to V-284
Dornier Do 27	V-601 to V-607
Pilatus PC-6 Porter	V-612 to V-635

Not all the aircraft listed will be operational, and gaps occur in the batches, but it will give an idea of the composition of types within the air arm. The wide dispersal of units around the country and the natural security cloak surrounding unit locations make squadron/code/base tie-ups difficult, but the basic formation is the squadron, with up to eight squadrons forming an Air Regiment.

Additional markings involve the application of the last three digits of the serial on the nose of the aircraft, as seen on the F-5s, while some of the Hunters have only the last two digits on the nose and on the nosewheel door. Maintenance markings are normally applied in French and German. Unit emblems are car-

ried on only two or three aircraft in each squadron but they serve to identify the unit. Examples are 17 Sqn (Mirages) which has a red diving bird on a white circle, 11 Sqn

Right: One of the 98 F-5E Tiger IIs bought by the Swiss and an integral part of the country's defenses. The subtle difference between the two shades of grey can be seen on the wings.

Syria

Supported and supplied with military aircraft and equipment by the Soviet Union, Syria has fared badly when flying in combat against Israel, despite having some of the most capable front-line types in service. The Syrian Arab Air Force is known as Al Quwwat al Jawwiya al Arabiya as'Souriya and operates MiG-21s, 23s, 25s and 29s in 12 interceptor regiments. The interdictor/attack element flies MiG-23BNs, Sukhoi Su-20/22s and the potent Su-24 Fencer. These machines carry the national marking shown above in the standard positions and have individual numbers, usually based on their construction numbers, located on the nose in Arabic characters. The tail flash is the national flag.

Above: To most people it is an F-5E, but to the Republic of China Air Force it is the Chung Cheng and 256 are being built in Taiwan to infuse some

(F-5Es) with a yellow tiger's head on a black circle, 10 Sqn (Mirage IIIRS) with a red/white bird's head in arrow style, and a black panther on a green shield on 18 Sqn Hunters.

Taiwan

In 1928 the Nationalist party in China adopted a new flag with a 12-pointed star, each point representing the two-hour period of the Chinese day. When the Nationalist forces of General Chiang Kai-shek were defeated by the Communist army of Mao Tse-tung in 1949, the survivors moved to the island of Formosa and set up the state of Nationalist China. Now called Taiwan, this state has established its own industry to supply the armed forces with helicopters (118 licence-built Bell UH-1H for the Army), jet trainers (60 AT-3S) and tactical fighters. Due to enter service in the mid-1990s, is the indigenous Ching Kuo light fighter, but accidents to the prototypes have held up this project. 256 F-5E Tiger IIs have been produced under the name Chung Cheng along with 52 two-seat F-5Fs. They currently serve with 11 squadrons of the Republic of China Air Force, formerly known as the Chinese Nationalist Air Force (Chung-kuo Kung Chuan), supplemented by more than 100 Lockheed F-104 Starfighters obtained from a number of different sources, mainly in Europe but including 27 TF-104Gs formerly used for Luftwaffe pilot training at Luke AFB, Arizona.

The star insignia is carried by all aircraft on the fuselage but only applied to the top surface of the F-5 wings. No tail flash is currently used, the only marking here being the aircraft serial number applied in white on the camouflage background colour. A four-digit code is prominently marked on the fuselage but this does not directly reflect the construction number — F-5E 400967 has 5110 on the fuselage, while 400968 has 5111 in a similar position; these were the tenth and eleventh aircraft, but 500334, the 55th example, carries 5161, as shown at left.

modernity into this Far East air arm. By the national marking is the aircraft number and on the fin is the US serial. The Chinese characters mean 'in the centre'.

Tanzania

When Tanganyika and Zanzibar united in 1964 to form the United Republic of Tanzania, elements from both flags were combined to form the national emblem which is displayed on the fins of aircraft operated by the Tanzanian People's Defence Force Air Wing (Jeshi la Wananchi la Tanzania). The 'torch of freedom' roundel is located on the wings of most of the aircraft and on the fuselage it normally splits the JW prefix and the three-digit serial. The full serial of four numerals is usually applied on the fins of transport aircraft such as the DHC-5D Buffalo (JW9019 to JW9024) and HS.748 (JW9008 to JW9010). All the serials seen to date have been in the 9000 range, but no information is available on the markings on Tanzania's few combat aircraft. These are all of Chinese origin, currently comprising 11 Xian F-7s, 10 Shenyang F-6s and eight F-5s.

Aircraft operated by the Tanzanian Police Air Wing and government machines carry civilian registrations prefixed 5H.

Thailand

After many years operating an almost bewildering mixture of types, many of them obsolete, the Royal Thai Air Force has embarked on a modernization programme which it hopes will forestall any attempt by troublesome countries to the east to invade it. Eighteen F-16A/Bs are in service, with a further 18 to follow in 1995, while 47 RFB Fantrainer 400/600s provide a modern training aircraft. The Northrop F-5Es already in service are painted in a disruptive 'aggressor' scheme of green, grey and light blue and carry miniature roundels on the rear fuselage, a small representation of the Thai flag on the fin and a five- digit serial number on the lower part of the fin. As with many Thai military aircraft, a separate number is carried by the F-5s as well as the serial; one example has 61670 on the fin and 10222 on the fuselage; the first three digits are thought to relate to the squadron number. The 1st Wing's F-5As have carried the unit's yellow and black leaping tiger on the forward fuselage; examples are F-5A 21257 and F-5B 38439.

The colours of the Thai flag are based on the Trairong ensign, introduced in 1917, in which red represents the nation, white the religion and blue the monarchy. On some aircraft, such as the C-130 Hercules, the roundel is applied in the US style, above the port wing and below the starboard, while on others (T-33s and SF.260s) it is above and below both wings. The fin flash is sometimes applied to the rudder rather than to the fin. Note that on Royal Thai Navy aircraft the tail flash comprises the official naval ensign, which incorporates a white elephant in its centre.

Numbering on Thai aircraft takes a variety of different forms. Sometimes the build number is used as the code for the machine such as the two Army-operated Shorts 330 aircraft 3098 and 3102 which are their production numbers. The application of different numbers from the serials has already been outlined above, while a third variation is the incorporation of the squadron number in the serial, an example being the Hercules of 601 Sqn — 60101, 60102 and 60103 — which were built as 4861, 4862 and 4863.

Thai language and numerals are often carried by support aircraft such as helicopters and transports, sometimes with the equivalent marking in English on the opposite side. Most maintenance markings are in English, signifying the large amount of US aid which has been given to Thailand over the past two decades.

0	1	2	3	4
0	๑	๒	๓	๔

5	6	7	8	9
๕	๖	๗	๘	๙

Togo

Originally German, more recently French, but independent since 1960, the Togo Republic uses the pan-African colours of red, yellow and green incorporating a white star signifying national purity. The flag is applied to the fin of aircraft flown by the Force Aérienne Togolaise and the roundel marking is carried on fuselage and wings. The sole combat capability is provided by five Dassault/Dornier AlphaJets, the most recent of which was an attrition replacement delivered in 1991; six Embraer EMB-326 Xavantes, and three armed SOCATA TB.30 Epsilons which are used for the COIN mission in addition to their training function. Aircraft are identified by civilian registrations applied on the rear fuselage. They are in the 5V-M series, the AlphaJets being 5V-MBA to 5V-MBE and carrying the last two letters of the registration in black on the side of the forward fuselage.

Tunisia

Based on the Turkish flag (Tunisia was under Turkish rule in the mid-nineteenth century), the present national emblem forms the circular marking carried by all aircraft flown by the Republic of Tunisia Air Force. No fin marking is carried. Independent from France since 1956, Tunisia has only a small air arm.

Interception and reconnaissance is the task of 14 F-5E Tiger IIs, while 18 Aermacchi MB.326B/KLs double as light attack/trainers. Eighteen SF.260CT/WT Warriors fly the COIN mission in addition to training duties. Combat aircraft are camouflaged in green/brown, while Warriors have dayglo orange noses, fin tips, tip tanks and a vertical band around the rear fuselage. Five figure serials are carried on the fin, prefixed Y for combat aircraft, Z for transports, W for trainers, and L for helicopters. Call signs, prefixed by TS, are carried on the fuselage.

Turkey

Part of NATO, Turkey is a recipient of large amounts of American aid to maintain the strength and effectiveness of the country's armed forces. Türk Hava Kuvvetleri is one of the main beneficiaries of this aid and its inventory includes F.16 C/Ds, F-104 Starfighters, F-4 Phantoms and F-5s. Many of the aircraft in combat ▶

use have been acquired from other air forces due to Turkey's poor financial situation. Of these, only the license-built F-16s, which are powered by GE's F110-100 turbofan, can be considered modern. In all, 160 are on order, 24 of which are two-seat D models, with completion by the end of 1994. They are replacing F-104G Starfighters.

Turkish military aircraft carry a fin flash duplicating the national flag and comprising a crescent moon and five-pointed star, traditional symbols of Islam. On the fuselage and wings, the original red Ottoman flag, outlined in white, was replaced in the early 1970s by the red and white roundel seen today. Individual aircraft identification is by its serial number if it is a former USAF or US Navy machine, or by the original construction number. A prefix digit is used to indicate the aircraft's base airfield. One example is an F-4E Phantom, whose serial 70295 is displayed in black at the base of the fin, with 1-295 in black outlined white on the intakes, the prefix indicating the base. Base numbers and names are: 1 Eskisehir; 2 Cigli; 3 Konya; 4 Murted; 5 Merzifon; 6 Bandirma; 7 Erhac; 8 Diyarbakir; 9 Balikesir; 12 Erkilet, 15 Istanbul.

Sometimes, as in the case of the 20 ex-Luftwaffe Transalls of 221 Sqn at Erkilet, the base code number and the serial are split by the roundel;

Above: Turkey became a member of the Phantom 'club' in 1974 and currently has more than 80 on strength. 01019 was the fourth F-4E delivered new from McDonnell Douglas and is shown before the application of unit codes and identification number to the engine intake. Camouflage is Vietnam style with night formation strips on nose, forward fuselage and fin.

these aircraft also have the construction number painted in black on a broad white band across the fin and rudder. Transport and support types such as the Bell UH-1H helicopters often carry the Air Force title in large letters on the fuselage. Badges do not feature on Turkish combat aircraft, but they have been seen on the Transalls, the T-37s of the training unit at Cigli and on some Army-operated helicopters. What was probably an unofficial marking seen on the nose of a Dakota participating in the Turkish invasion of Cyprus in 1974 was a light blue outline of the island with three yellow parachutes superimposed. Turkish military aircraft wear various camouflage schemes, with many machines retaining the colours of their previous owner. Browns and tans are shades most favoured when aircraft are re-painted, though there appears to be no set scheme for any particular type.

United Arab Emirates

In 1971 seven small states around the Persian Gulf combined to form the United Arab Emirates. They were Abu Dhabi, Dubai, Amman, Fujairah, Ras al-Kaimah, Sharjah and Umm al-Qaiwan: all contribute to the funding of the Air Force, and the new joint flag is carried by all military aircraft operated by the United Arab Emirates Air Force. Most UAEAF aircraft are based in Abu Dhabi, which is also the headquarters, and Dubai. The combat element operates 35 Mirage 2000s, comprising 21 2000E interceptors, eight 2000R reconnaissance aircraft, and six two seat 2000D conversion trainers, backed by 29 survivors of the original 32 Mirage 5AD/RAD/DADs received in 1977.

The Mirages are painted in desert camouflage and carry serials in batches according to the version. For example Mirage 5AD and 5EAD fighter-bombers 401-412 and 501-514; reconnaissance Mirage 5RADs 601-603; and Mirage 5DAD trainers 201-203. These numbers are applied in black on the aircraft nose and repeated in Arabic characters, and when delivered the machines

also carried A.D.A.F. alongside the roundel on the intake sides. The Mirage 2000s are operated by II Shaheen Squadron, based at Al Dhafra, while the others are with I Shaheen Squadron at Sharjah. BAe Hawk T.63s have been received to update the training force, the 16 aircraft bearing serials 1001-1016 and being assigned to the Abu Dhabi element of the UAEAF. A further 12 more advanced Hawk 100s are currently on order.

Dubai, further along the coast, has the same markings as Abu Dhabi; it has operated handful of MB.326s, both single- and two-seaters, for some years in the training and light attack roles. They carry large white serials 201-208 on the rear fuselage and are supplemented by five MB.339s. Eight Hawk T.61 are in service marked 501-508. Carrying the full UAEAF insignia are the DHC-5D Buffalo transports which carry the title on one side of the fuselage roundel and the Arabic equivalent on the other. The six aircraft, 306-311, have the serials on the nose and rear fuselage and also under the wings.

Below: As part of the UAE armed forces, the Western Air Command (formerly Abu Dhabi Air Force) operates 16 Hawk T.63 advanced trainers at Al Dhafra. Colours are sand and light brown on the upper surface and light grey undersurfaces

United Kingdom

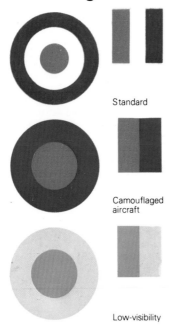

Standard

Camouflaged aircraft

Low-visibility

Markings and insignia of the British Services are many and varied and have prompted publication of a number of books devoted to the subject. This section deals only with the current markings applied to front-line aircraft operated by the Royal Air Force and the Royal Navy's Fleet Air Arm. Of all the insignia, the red, white and blue roundel has remained the symbol of British air power since its adoption by the Royal Flying Corps on December 11, 1914. It replaced the Union Flag on the fuselage sides and under the wings, and was a reversal of the French roundel. Six months later, in June 1915, red, white and blue rudder striping was introduced, setting the general pattern and positioning for British Service aircraft to the present day. Of course there have been variations in roundel size, application, style and location but the basic marking is still carried.

The application of markings and camouflage on UK military aircraft is specified and approved by the Ministry of Defence acting on behalf of the user service, and any change or modification has to be officially approved, or at least tentatively agreed down to squadron or unit level. Current orders state:

'Roundels are to be applied to the top and bottom surfaces of both main planes and on each side of the fuselage. A fin flash is to be applied to both sides of the fin. As an exception, roundel may be omitted from the undersurface of the mainplanes of tanker aircraft and the fin flash may be omitted from gliders constructed from plastic type materials.' In addition, 'aircraft serial numbers are to be applied on both sides of the fuselage'.

Roundel colours

The roundels on today's RAF front-line aircraft have had the white removed to form what is generally, but unofficially and incorrectly known as a B Type roundel, comprising red and blue with the former occupying half the diameter. Basic colours are matt or lustreless Post Office Red (BS381C-538) and Roundel Blue (-110), but to reduce marking visibility matt Pink and Pale Blue have been authorized to replace the original brighter shades. Roundel sizes vary according to aircraft type, but they are standardized at 54in (1,372mm), 48in (1,219mm), 36in (914mm), 18in

(457mm) and 12in (305mm) diameter overall. There are exceptions and changes will occur.

Fin flashes follow the same colour shades as the roundels and are usually located on the continuation of the fuselage top line, with the rear edge coinciding with the rear edge of the fin. The Jaguar provides a good example of this official requirement, while the Buccaneer and Phantom have their flash applied toward the top and near the leading edge respectively. Note that this type of marking is not displayed on Royal Navy or Army aircraft.

Serial numbers form the basis of aircraft identification in the British Services. The practice began in 1912, initially embracing aircraft of both the Royal Flying Corps and the Naval Wing and expanding subsequently to include the Army, and numbering has continued ever since. The present system consists of three digits in the 100 to 999 range, prefixed by two letters (AA to ZZ); a recent RAF example is ZE157, a Panavia Tornado F.3 fighter, but the range had reached ZH200 by mid-1990. All types of military aircraft are included, together with Service-operated hovercraft, and as a security measure there are gaps in the numbering to prevent accurate assessment of UK air strength. RAF aircraft are re-

quired to carry their serial number on each side of the rear fuselage or, in the case of the Tornado fighter, on the lower portion of the fin, forward of the flash. Standard serial height is 8in (203mm), usually in white on the current grey fighter scheme or black on the grey/green finish. Until the 1970s and the adoption of grey camouflage on RAF aircraft, almost all aircraft had their serials repeated on the lower surfaces of the wings. Some still do, particularly the larger types, but the accumulation of underwing weapons, fuel tanks and special purpose pods, all hung on pyons, obscured the serial to such an extent that it is beginning to disappear from combat aircraft such as the Phantom and Tornado fighter. On the other hand, Tornado strike aircraft retain the serial in black on the lower surfaces of the tailplanes. On the starboard side the tops of the letters and figures are nearest to the leading edge; on the port side, the tops are nearest to the trailing edge.

Phantom serials

An example of the serialling allocated to RAF combat aircraft is provided by the various blocks used for the McDonnell Douglas F-4 Phantom. This aircraft was ordered for both the RN (as the FG.1) and the RAF (FGR.2), but with the withdrawal of the last conventional carrier in 1979 all operational Phantoms were taken over by the latter Service. Phantom FG.1: XT595-598, XT857-876, XV565-592; Phantom FGR.2: XT852, XT853, XT891-914, XV393-442, XV460-501; Phantom F-4J (UK) ZE350-ZE364. Only two Phantom squadrons remain in service in 1992; Nos 56 and 74, both equipped with FGR.2s and based at Wattisham, while No 1435 Flight, also with FGR.2s, is operational from Mount Pleasant in the Falkland Islands. The discarded FG.1s and F-4Js are currently in store. They will soon be followed by the remaining FGR.2s, as Nos 56 and 74 squadron are scheduled to disband during 1993. ▶

Left: Two Tornado GR.1s of 31 Sqn on exercise, identified by the green and yellow flash on the nose and the star on the tail.

British service aircraft designations provide an indication as to the role of the various types in use. The current list of functional prefixes is shown in the table, the abbreviation being followed by the Mark number, normally shortened to Mk, but more often than not replaced by a full point, as in Harrier GR.3:

UK aircraft designations

AEW	Airborne Early Warning
AH	Army Helicopter
AL	Army Liaison
AS	Anti-Submarine
B	Bomber
B(I)	Bomber (Interdictor)
B(K)	Bomber (Tanker)
B(PR)	Bomber (Photo Reconnaissance)
C	Transport
CC	Transport and Communications
D	Drone or unmanned aircraft
E	Electronic/Flight check
F	Fighter
FG	Fighter Ground Attack
FGA	Fighter Ground Attack
FGR	Fighter Ground Attack Reconnaissance
FR	Fighter Reconnaissance
FRS	Fighter Reconnaissance Strike
GA	Ground Attack
GR	Ground Attack Reconnaissance
HAR	Helicopter Air Rescue
HAS	Helicopter Anti-Submarine
HC	Helicopter Cargo
HT	Helicopter Training
HU	Helicopter Utility
K	Tanker
MR	Maritime Reconnaissance
PR	Photo Reconnaissance
R	Reconnaissance
S	Strike
T	Trainer
TT	Target Towing
TX	Training Glider
W	Weather

In addition to the aircraft serial, individual machines within a squadron carry a one- or two-letter code on the fin. This is either in a single colour (black, white, yellow or red) or in an outlined style (dark green outlined in yellow for 27 Sqn Tornados). Operational Conversion Units use a number of variations to distinguish their aircraft, including the three digits of the serial number, a sequential series of numbers usually beginning at 01, a code letter on each side of the fuselage roundel or, in the case of the Trinational Tornado Training Establishment, a letter and two digits.

Badges are a part of squadron tradition in many countries and the RAF is no exception. It maintains its past honours by retaining some kind of unit emblem on its aircraft despite the official requirement not to compromise the tone-down camouflage effect. Chequers, flashes, birds of prey and bars of colour help to brighten the dullness of the present-day finishes, but even before they are applied provision is made to ensure that they would disappear overnight should the need ever arise. Noses, engine intakes and fins are the usual location for this type of marking and some examples are illustrated. The present list of RAF front-line combat squadrons and their insignia is included here for completeness, but is only intended as an *aide mémoire* to enable a unit to be identified quickly and, it is hoped, accurately. There are many other squadrons in the RAF which have a combat role in wartime, such as the OCUs and Weapons Units, and it should be borne in mind that most markings are subject to change due to operational circumstances.

Maintenance and rescue

Other markings carried by front-line aircraft can be noted by walking round an example. Maintenance and rescue stencilling instructions are the most obvious, while less prominent are such essential items as wing-walk lines to prevent damage to moving parts and the small DTD paint specification numbers which usually occur at various points over the airframe. Some of the main NATO maintenance markings are illustrated in this section and can be found on aircraft operated by many of the world's military aircraft. The symbols are generally 4in (102mm) in their longest direction with the inscription in block capitals and numerals 1.5in (38mm) high except where otherwise specified. ▶

RAF operational, emergency and safety markings

Explosive actuated device

Variation for RAF Germany

Emergency canopy or hatch release controls

Fuselage break-in points

Fire access panels

Emergency equipment stowage

Powerplant inlet and/or exhaust

First aid kit stowage

Note that aircraft permanently based in West Germany have much stencilling duplicated in the German language; sometimes complete safety instructions are applied to RAFG aircraft. Pilot's names are occasionally carried, mainly by the Unit Commanders, whose aircraft also have small rank pennants applied around the cockpit area (eg, two red horizontal stripes on light blue outlined in a dark blue arrow head for a Wing Commander).

Sea Harrier markings

Royal Navy Sea Harriers carry all the standard NATO markings, but there are some differences in national insignia compared with that applied to RAF aircraft. The most obvious is the lack of fin flashes, officially decreed not to be applied. In their place is the title ROYAL NAVY in 6in (152mm) high black letters along the base and under the squadron emblem, which is also in black outline form. At the fin tip is the carrier code letter, which varies according to which two of the three carriers are operational at the time, the two Sea Harrier squadrons being based accordingly. Each aircraft of the unit carries a three-digit number on the intake.

The badges comprise crossed swords within an 'arrow' marking (800 Sqn), a trident (801 Sqn) and a winged fist (899 Sqn). Serials on Sea Harriers are difficult to find if you don't know where to look. They are actually located on the lower fin in black 3in (76mm) high letters and numbers in the XZ and ZA prefix ranges. Roundels have undergone a number of different styles since the Falklands war, but they appear to have standardised at 18in (457mm) in four positions — either side of the engine intakes and on the top surface of the wings. Note that like RAF aircraft Sea Harriers no longer carry underwing serials or roundels.

Army Air Corps

The army operates a few Beaver and Defender fixed wing aircraft and around 120 helicopters, namely Scouts, Gazelles and Lynxes. Scouts and Gazelles are used for transport and liaison, while the Lynxes fulfil a dual transport and anti-tank role. Until the early 1990s, army aircraft were painted in a dark green and black camouflage scheme, but Gazelles and Lynxes have recently been appearing in a pale grey and green pattern. Helicopters have the word ARMY in black on their tail boom, together with their serial number.

Below: RAF Hawks in three different colour schemes. The light grey T.1A is from No.1 Tactical Weapons Unit, which acts as a close-range air defence squadron in time of war. The grey/green aircraft is also from the same unit, while the red/white machine is from No.4 FTS.

All British heavy transport helicopters are flown by units of the Royal Air Force or the Royal Navy. These machines include Boeing-Vertol Chinooks HC.1, Westland Pumas HC.1 and Westland Sea Kings HC.4.

Above: A RAF Phantom from 111 Squadron, which has since re-equipped with Tornado F.3s. The badge and lightning flash are clear in this view, as is the pale grey air superiority scheme.

RAF front-line combat squadrons

Squadron	Aircraft	Identification marks
1 Sqn	Harrier GR.7/T.10	Winged 1 in white circle on nose
2 Sqn	Tornado GR.1A	Black 2 in white triangle on fin
3 Sqn	Harrier GR.7/T.10	Red & Green cockatrice on white circle and green/yellow bars
4 Sqn	Harrier GR.7/T.10	Red 4 with gold lightning flash on nose
5 Sqn	Tornado F.3	Green maple leaf on white circle
6 Sqn	Jaguar GR.1A/T.2A	Red can opener in circle; red zig-zag on fin
9 Sqn	Tornado GR.1	Dark green bat on fin
11 Sqn	Tornado F.3	One red, one yellow hawk on fin
12 Sqn	Tornado GR.1	Fox's head on engine intakes
13 Sqn	Tornado GR.1A	Black Lynx head on dagger on white shield
14 Sqn	Tornado GR.1	Winged emblem between blue & white bars
17 Sqn	Tornado GR.1	Black & white arrow head on nose
23 Sqn	Tornado F.3	Red eagle
25 Sqn	Tornado F.3	Hawk on gauntlet
29 Sqn	Tornado F.3	Red Xs on white background on nose and fin
31 Sqn	Tornado GR.1	Green & yellow arrow on nose; yellow star on fin
41 Sqn	Jaguar GR.1A/T.2A	Red cross of Lorraine on fin and intake
43 Sqn	Tornado F.3	Black & white checks on fin
54 Sqn	Jaguar GR.1A/T.2A	Blue & yellow checks on intake
111 Sqn	Tornado F.3	Black lightning flash outlined yellow
617 Sqn	Tornado GR.1	Red lightning flash on black fin band

United States of America

Standard

Low-visibility

Above: This F-111 has its serial and vital maintenance data stencilled under the cockpit.

Below Left: The letters 'LN' on the tail of this F-111 show that it is from the 48th FW, based at Lakenheath in England.

Fifty states and the District of Columbia, which includes the capital city of Washington, are represented by the stars in the corner of the national flag of the United States, while the 13 stripes signify the original 13 colonies that rebelled against the British in 1775. Although the national flag is seldom carried in its entirety on US military front-line aircraft, the star and bar emblem forms the basic insignia for all US military types and was adopted in its current form in 1947. Construction of the national marking shape, using Insignia Red, Insignia White and Insignia Blue colours, is carefully formulated using the diameter of the circle, which is standardized in multiples of 5in (127mm); from this the sizes of the bars or rectangles and the five- pointed star are calculated.

Technical Orders for the application of this marking or variations of it state that it is to be located on 'each side of the aircraft fuselage, mid-way between the wing trailing edge and the leading edge of the stabilizer' and on the upper surface of the left wing and on the lower surface of the right wing'. These instructions are interpreted in various ways depending on the aircraft: the F-15 Eagle has the insignia on the fuselage, but adjacent to the variable angle intake, as does the F-111, while the shape of the F-16 dictates its application on the rear fuselage and in inconspicuous outline form. In fact, the three colours associated with the marking are being used less and less as a result of the general toning-down process currently fashionable on combat aircraft of many nations. Shadow grey or black outlines are widely used, and until recently, when selected USN units started to break the mould, hardly any bright colours were used externally on American aircraft.

To understand US military aircraft markings it is as well to outline how US designations are arrived at. Every aircraft introduced into service is given a number in the sequence of the type's role, a prefix letter indicating the role, a further letter after the model number to show the subtype; the full designation also includes a block number and the initials of the manufacturer. For example F-111E can be deduced as the 111th fighter design and the fifth model (E) developed. The following type letters are currently in use (examples are given in the table).

US type designations

A	Tactical support or attack (A-10)
B	Bomber (B-1)
C	Transport (C-130)
E	Electronic aircraft (E-3)
F	Fighter (F-111)
H	Helicopter (H-3)
O	Observation (O-2)
P	Patrol (P-3)
S	Anti-submarine (S-3)
T	Trainer (T-38)
U	Utility (U-17)
V	V/Stol (V-22)
X	Experimental (X-29)

Letters used as prefixes to the basic type indicators listed above such as DC-130 include the following:

US role prefixes

D	Drone director
E	Electronic equipment
H	Search and rescue
K	Tanker
L	Cold-weather operations
M	Permanently modified
N	Assigned special tests
Q	Drone
R	Reconnaissance
V	Staff transport
W	Weather reconnaissance
Y	Service test
Z	Project

The official aircraft designation can be found in an Aircraft Data Legend usually applied in black 1in (25mm) high letters on the left-hand side of the forward fuselage adjacent to the cockpit. This gives the type, model and series, the serial number, the aircraft production block number and the grade of fuel specified for the machine. Note that the manufacturer's or popular names for aircraft are specifically prohibited from use or display on any Air Force aircraft. Thus the name Eagle will not be found applied on the outside airframe of an F-15.

Aircraft serial numbers are allotted to USAF and US Army machines on a Fiscal Year (FY) basis, a system which has been in use since 1920. The FY runs from July 1 to June 30 and each serial has a two-digit prefix showing the year in which the aircraft, helicopter or even missile was ordered, followed by up to five digits which form the individual serial within that year's allocations. An example is General Dynamics FB-111A, serial number 67-7193 which was ordered in FY 1967 and was the 7193rd vehicle ordered in that year. The full serial appears small under the cockpit, but it is also applied on the fin in slightly abbreviated form as ▶

77193 in light grey on a dark green background colour.

Tail presentation takes a number of forms. Aircraft used by the former Tactical Air Command (superceded in 1992 by Air Combat Command), plus USAFE and PACAF machine have the FY numbers in small digits beneath the letters AF, both in 6in (152mm) high characters, with the last three of the serial in 15in (381mm) high digits. Usually applied in black on grey or camouflaged surfaces, the sizes change with the aircraft, some types having the large number in 6in or 8in (203mm) high digits. Sometimes four numbers of the serial are carried or the last digit of the FY and the first of the serial are presented small under the AF followed by the last three of the serial. The user designator USAF is applied on some aircraft fins, while larger types such as KC-135 tankers carry U.S. AIR FORCE along the nose in prominent characters; support and training aircraft also have this style of identity.

In addition to the serial, USAF combat aircraft carry two-letter tail codes. Introduced on tactical aircraft during the Vietnam war to aid identification of an aircraft's unit and base, the system has been retained and in general each code forms an abbreviation of the unit's base name, although this is not always the case. On most tactical aircraft, the letters are applied in 24in (610mm) high characters, usually in black but occasionally in grey or even white. For example the letters on the Cessna OA-37 are 8in high due to the relatively small area available, while those on the C-130 Hercules were 36in (914mm). Orders state that the code will not overlap onto the rudder and where possible will avoid access panels, aerials and other markings on the fin. The current list of codes provides a guide to aircraft type, base and unit (pages 112-113).

Badges and unit insignia used by the USAF, and indeed the US Navy and Marine Corps as well, are a subject that is impossible to cover in any depth in a book of this size. Officially, USAF aircraft carry the badge of the user Command. SAC and TAC emblems are still carried as at early 1992, although these commands have now been amalgamated as Air Combat Command, and will presumably be replaced by new insignia in due course, although USAFE and PACAF should remain current.

US Air Force tail codes

AK	21 FW/343 FW	F-15/A-10	Eielson/Elmendorf
AL	187 FG	F-16	Donnelly Field
AZ	162 FG	F-16	Tucson
BA	67 RW	RF-4C	Bergstrom
BC	110 ASG	OA-37/A-10	Battle Creek
BD	917 FG	A-10	Barksdale
BH	117 RW	RF-4C	Birmingham
BT	36 FW	F-15	Bitburg (Germany)
CC	27 FW	F-111	Cannon
CO	140 FW	A-7	Buckley
CR	32 FG	F-15	Soesterberg (Netherlands)
CT	103 FG	A-10	Bradley
DC	113 FW	F-16	Andrews
DM	355 TW	A-10	Davis-Monthan
DO	906 FG	F-16	Wright Patterson
ED	6510 TW	various	Edwards
EG	33 FW	F-15	Eglin
EL	23 FW	A-10	England
ET	3246 TW	various	Eglin
FF	1 FW	F-15	Langley
FM	482 FW	F-16	Homestead
FS	188 FW	F-16	Fort Smith
FW	122 FW	F-4	Fort Wayne
GA	35 FW	F-4	George
GU	460 RW	RF-4	Taegu (Korea)

HA	185 FG	A-7	Sioux City
HF	181 FG	F-4	Hulman Field
HI	419 FW	F-16	Hill
HL	388 FW	F-16	Hill
HO	49 FW	F-15	Holloman
HS	31 FW	F-16	Homestead
IA	132 FW	F-16	Des Moines
IL	182 ASG	OA-37	Peoria
IN	930 FG	A-10	Grissom
IS	57 FS	F-15	Keflavik (Iceland)
KC	442 FW	A-10	Richards-Gebaur
LA	405 TW	F-15	Luke
LF	58 FW	F-16	Luke
LN	48 FW	F-111	Lakenheath (UK) until '93
LR	944 FG	F-16	Luke
LY	48 FS	F-15	Langley
MA	104 FG	A-10	Barnes
MB	354 FW	A-10	Myrtle Beach
MC	56 TW	F-16	MacDill
MD	175 FG	A-10	Martin
MI	127 FW	F-16	Selfridge
MJ	432 FW	F-16	Misawa (Japan)
MO	366 FW	F-111/EF-111	Mountain Home
MY	347 FW	F-16	Moody
NF	602 ACW	OA-10	Davis-Monthan
NJ	108 FW	F-4	McGuire
NO	926 FG	A-10	New Orleans
NT	232 FTW	T-43	Mather
NY	174 FW	F-16	Hancock Field
OH	121 FW	A-7	Rickenbacker
OH	178 FG	A-7	Springfields
OH	180 FG	A-7	Toledo
OK	138 FG	A-7	Tulsa
OS	51 FW	F-16/A-10	Osan (South Korea)
OT	AWC	various	Eglin
PA	111 ASG	OA-10	Willow Grove
PR	156 FG	A-7	Puerto Rico
PT	112 FG	A-7	Greater Pittsburg
RS	86 FW	F-16	Ramstein (Germany)
SA	149 FG	F-16	Kelly
SB	66 ECW	EC-130	Sembach (Germany)
SD	114 FG	A-7	Joe Foss
SH	507 FG	F-16	Tinker
SI	183 FG	F-16	Springfield
SJ	4 FW	F-15	Seymour Johnson
SL	131 FW	F-4	Bridgetown
SP	52 FW	F-4G/F-16	Spangdahlem (Germany)
SR	507 ACW	OA-10	Shaw
SW	363 FW	F-16	Shaw
TF	301 FW	F-16	Carswell
TR	37 FW	F-117	Tonopah
TX	924 FG	F-16	Bergstrom
TY	325 TW	F-15	Tyndall
UH	20FW/66ECM	F-111/EF-111	Upper Heyford (UK) until 1993
VA	192 FG	A-7	Byrd Field
WA	57 FWW	various	Nellis
WI	128 FW	A-10	Truax Field
WP	8 FW	F-16	Kunsan (South Korea)
WW	35 FW	F-4G	George
ZZ	18 FW	RF-4C/F-15	Kadena (Okinawa)

Above: The tail codes on these F-16s show that they were ordered in FY 1981 and that they currently belong to the 388th FW at Hill AFB.

Below: AK signifies that these F-15As belong to the 21st FW at Elmendorf. This picture is unusual in that the four aircraft wear consecutive serials.

Representative F-15 squadron badges

**1st FW, 12th AF,
Langley AFB, Virginia**

**36th FW, 17th AF,
Bitburg, Germany**

**33rd FW, 9th AF,
Eglin AFB, Florida**

These are usually located on the fin in 10in (254mm) or 18in (457mm) decals. In addition, the individual squadron or wing badge is carried, often with further embellishments such as coloured stripes across the fin, squadron emblems, individual and certainly unofficial squadron markings of all shapes and sizes. Many flamboyant insignia are only for competitions such as Gunsmoke, Flag exercises or other 'friendly' tactical operations. Air National Guard units generally carry the official ANG emblem and a distinctive a coloured stripe across the fin. Air Force Reserve units carry 'AFRES' in black on dark camouflage to conform with tone-down requirements. However, not all badges are in full colour. Like

Above: The 1st, 33rd and 36th FWs were, respectively, the first operational F-15 unit, the first with MSIP F-15Cs and the first overseas F-15 wing.

the AFRES markings, some insignia are in black outline only. Following a shakeup in 1991, USAF Commands have undergone a thorough restructuring. Strategic Air Command has been dissolved, and its combat aircraft allocated to TAC to form the new Air Combat Command (ACC), while Military Airlift Command has been expanded by the addition of tankers formerly operated by SACs 15th Air Force to become the new Air Mobility Command (AMC). Air National Guard (ANG) and Air Force Reserve (AFRes) units are allocated to either depending on their equipment, the latter accounting for over half the total airlift capability.

Other markings on USAF aircraft include pilot and crew chief names usually and officially applied on the left-hand side of the front fuselage below the cockpit in 2in (51mm) high black letters, but again this varies between units and even aircraft. Maintenance stencilling is in accord with NATO-agreed standards with basic instructional markings as shown in the UK section. Rescue and emergency markings continue to remain prominent although greys and black have sometimes replaced white and yellow to reduce visibility at distance.

Many Air Force aircraft carry a pattern of parallel lines and rules near the refuelling receptacle. This shape helps the boom operator on the tanker by providing visual cues to the ▶

exact position of the probe as it is nearing the receptacle. On some types the design is relatively simple, but on others it can be large and complex. The B-1B has a prominent pattern above the nose which was originally painted in black, but the current scheme is in white.

Interestingly, Vietnam air ace Randy Cunningham has often said that many pilots would like a simple large number (rather like the Soviet 'bort' number) painted on the side of US fighters to help them quickly identify friendly callsigns in the confusion of a dogfight.

Navy and Marine Corps
Markings on USN and USMC combat aircraft have succumbed to the official tone-down requirements to the extent that the red, white and blue of the national insignia have been replaced by a grey outline over the Compass Grey background colour, rendering it almost impossible to see at anything more than a few yards. A return to earlier bright tail markings was observed in some carrier units during 1991, notably on board the USS *Independence*. In a close range 'furball' this has the advantage of giving instant identification, and may well be a clue to revised thinking by the USN. USN serials are generally known as Bureau Numbers (BuNos) and are allotted in sequence with up to six digits on current aircraft. They are not as prominent as those applied to USAF machines being located on the aft fuselage in small black or dark grey figures. Above the BuNo is the aircraft designation.

More prominent are the tail codes carried by USN/USMC aircraft, but these differ from those on USAF types. Navy codes signify the Carrier Air Wing (CVW) to which the aircraft is attached, and by implication the squadron. Although there are variations, the average CVW is composed of two fighter squadrons (VF) with 24 F-14A Tomcats; two fighter/attack (VFA) squadrons with 24 F/A-18 Hornets, one medium attack squadron (VA) with 10 or 11 A-6E Intruders; one tactical EW squadron (VAQ) with four EA-6B Prowlers; one AEW squadron (VAW) with four E-2C Hawkeyes; one ASW squadron (VS) with ten S-3A Vikings; and one helicopter ASW squadron (HS) with six SH-3H Sea Kings. There are currently 12 Air Wings operational, although this number looks set to be reduced further as defence cuts start to take effect in the future.

USAF B-1B

The dark radar absorbent colours on the B-1B give the aircraft a particularly sinister appearance. Markings are few and those that are present are mostly small and unobtrusive.

Breaking the sombre scheme are the air refuelling guide markings on the nose, the wing-walk lines and the single national emblem.

Air Wing designations

The carriers and their Air Wings are divided into two Fleets, Atlantic and Pacific; the former have squadrons carrying codes prefixed A, while the Pacific units have N prefixes. The codes take many styles depending on the individual units, but the main ones and their carrier or shore base are listed below.

Carrier Air Wing tail codes

AA	USS *Saratoga*
AB	USS *America*
AC	USS *John F Kennedy*
AD	Shore-based at Oceana, Key West and Cecil Field
AF	Shore-based at Dallas, Cecil Field, New Orleans and Atlanta
AG	USS *Dwight D Eisenhower*
AJ	USS *Theodore Roosevelt*
ND	Shore-based at Miramar, Alameda and Point Mugu
NE	USS *Kitty Hawk*
NF	USS *Midway*
NG	USS *Ranger*
NH	USS *Abraham Lincoln*
NJ	Shore-based at Miramar, Lemoore and Whidbey Island
NK	USS *Independence*
NL	USS *Carl Vinson*
NM	Shore-based at Lemoore

Individual aircraft carry a three-digit number on the nose with the last two digits repeated on the fin; the number is also repeated on the flaps for ident during launching. These are in black or dark grey and are often outlined in white. The word NAVY or MARINES identifies the user Service, this being applied towards the rear of the airframe. Squadron numbers are usually adjacent to the operator's name in the style 'VF-154'. The words JET IN-TAKE DANGER are applied in the appropriate position, previously in white and red but now in grey. The rescue and ejection seat triangle follow suit in the dullness of today's markings. Squadron insignia have for years in in subdued, shadowy greys, but as noted earlier, a return to brighter markings now seems in prospect.

US Marine Corps aircraft carry the legend MARINES to identify the user: on the AV-8B Harrier II it is located on the base of the fin and on the top ▶

Below: The first EF-111A Raven to be deployed to Europe, this machine illustrates the overall light grey finish and minimal low visibility markings worn by these powerful electronic warfare support aircraft.

surfaces of the right-hand wing. National insignia are carried in outline form and all Marine types have the unit number with a prefix which incorporates the letter M such as VMAT 203 for the AV-8B training unit.

Tail codes are carried, but are not abbreviations of the base name as in the USAF codes. Examples are CJ, belonging to HMH-461, a CH-53E unit and VL, belonging to VMA-331 who fly AV-8Bs.

US Navy F/A-18 markings

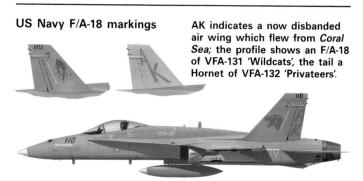

AK indicates a now disbanded air wing which flew from *Coral Sea;* the profile shows an F/A-18 of VFA-131 'Wildcats', the tail a Hornet of VFA-132 'Privateers'.

Representative F/A-18 squadron badges

VFA-113 'Stingers', USS *Independence*

VMFA-314 'Black Knights', MCAS El Toro

VFA-131 'Wildcats', USS *Eisenhower*

Uruguay

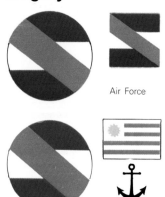

Air Force

Navy

This Spanish-speaking nation relies heavily on US aid for its military forces and this is manifest in particular in the Fuerza Aérea Uruguaya.

The main combat equipment comprises six Cessna A-37B light attack jets and five Lockheed AT-33s supplemented by six Argentinian Pucarás. The national circular marking is applied to the top surface of the port wing and the under surface of the starboard wing. In modified shape it is also carried on the rudder, sometimes extending the full length as on the Cessna T-41Ds and Beech T-34Bs, and as a small rectangle on the Cessna A-37 Dragonfly attack aircraft.

The FAU serialling system follows an accepted pattern: 001-099 for helicopters; 100-199 bombers; 200-299 fighters/advanced trainers; 300-399 trainers; 400-499 unused at present; 500-599 transports; 600-699 primary trainers; 700-799 communications types; 800-899

miscellaneous types. Numbers are applied both at the rear of the fuselage and at the nose on the A-37s and T-33s. Naval aircraft have the national flag on their tails, an anchor and national marking on the wings, with the legend ARMADA on the rear fuselage.

Above: Top view of a Uruguayan AF A-37B light attack aircraft showing the camouflage pattern and the stencilling, the latter mainly consisting of 'no step' and 'no push' instructions in Spanish. Note the small rudder marking and the single roundel.

Venezuela

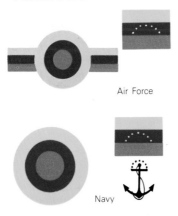

Air Force

Navy

Oil has been the saviour of Venezuela's economy and the high value of the commodity in the 1970s enabled the country's military forces to modernise, with the result that today Venezuela's air force (Fuerza Aérea Venezolana) is one of the most modern in Latin America. The FAV's fighter elements comprise two Escuadron or squadrons with GD F-16s, two with Mirage 50 EV/DVs, and two with Canadair CF-5s, making a total of some 50 aircraft. Four-

teen Rockwell OV-10E Broncos fly the counter-insurgency mission, while a further 18 may be acquired. They are supported in the COIN mission by T-2E Buckeyes.

Markings on FAV combat aircraft take the form of the insignia seen left with types such as the Mirage and Bronco having the roundel applied in the US style standard positions — fuselage sides, port upper wing and starboard lower wing. The standard tail fin marking comprises yellow/blue/red horizontal stripes, with seven white stars on the central blue band representing the number of provinces that formed the Venezuelan Federation in 1911.

The serialling of Venezuelan military aircraft appears to take a somewhat haphazard form. For instance, individual Mirages are 1297, 7162 and 9510. Some aircraft carry the air force initials FAV on the starboard top and port lower wing positions, and they are also applied to the rear boom of Bell helicopters operated by the Service. Transports have FUERZA AEREA VENEZOLANA on the fuselage. Maintenance ▶

and safety stencilling over the airframe is usually applied in Spanish such as RESCATE for Rescue.

The fixed wing transport force is based on six Aeritalia G.222 cargo aircraft and the same number of larger C-130 Hercules. A number of light communications aircraft are flown, including Gulfstreams, Citations, Learjets, Dassault-Breguet Falcons and Beech King Airs. A single Boeing 737 is used in the VIP transport role.

The Venezuelan Navy can claim no front-line combat types, but does field four C.212-200As Aviocars in the maritime patrol/anti-submarine role. These carry standard roundel and bar insignia on wings and fuselage with the legend MARINA in large letters on the rear fuselage. Escuadron

Above: One of Venezuela's two Mirage 5DV trainers displaying serial 5471 under the fin flash, two ejection seat triangles and the maker's name on the nose.

AS-01 operates the Aviocars, with four digit serials in the 0100 range; Escuadron TR-02 operates fixed wing transport aircraft, numbered from 0201, while Escuadron AS-03 flies Augusta-Bell 212 ASW helicopters, with serials from 0301. Aircraft in naval use also have a small anchor marking as well as the standard fin flash. Army-operated aircraft can be identified by an EV (Ejercito Venezolano) prefix to a four-digit serial, of which the first two indicate the year of purchase and the second two a sequential number.

Vietnam

Since the downfall of the South Vietnamese government in 1975 the unified Sociliast Republic of Vietnam has endeavoured to spread its influence in surrounding countries. The Vietnamese People's Air Force is part of the Army and has received an influx of modernized equipment in the form of MiG-23s and Sukhoi Su-22s, probably in exchange for the use of air and naval bases by the Soviet Forces. The yellow and red star and bar marking is usually applied on the fuselage and both surfaces of each wing, at least on the MiG-21s in service. Individual aircraft numbers consist of four digits applied on the nose, examples being 4326 and 5063 painted in red on the bare metal surface.

Some F.5A/Es and A-37Bs inherited from the Americans may still be in service.

Yemen

Following an agreement in 1981 for the North and South Yemen to merge, failure to agree details delayed unification to 1990, when the amalgamation of these two small Arab countries finally took place. The Unified Yemeni Arab Air Force uses the insignia of the North; a red, white and black roundel with a small green star in the white circle. The fin flash is a replica of the national flag. Equipment is mainly of Soviet origin, with 25 MiG-23BN Floggers and 70 or so MiG-21F/MF/bis Fishbed interceptors, with 50 Sukhoi Su-22BK/M Fitters in the attack role. Also on strength are a number of MiG-17F Frescos and a handful of F-5E Tiger IIs, both of doubtful serviceability. As the North Yemen air arm appears to have been dominant in the merger,

it seems probable that its serialling system has been retained. These normally consist of four digits, often in Arabic characters.

An example is Lockheed Hercules 1160, with roman numerals in black on the nose and both roman and arabic digits on the fin. The words YEMEN ARAB REPUBLIC AIR FORCE are on the fuselage of the same aircraft, in both Arabic and English.

Two C-130 Hercules and a few F-27 Friendships and Shorts Skyvans are the only western aircraft in the fixed wing transport fleet. Around 20 Soviet-built transports are in service, comprising a mixture of An-12s, An-26 and An-24s. Rotary wing assets are a similar mixture, with Mil Mi-8s and Mi-4s operating alongside AB-212s, AB-204s, Alouette IIIs and AB-206B Jetrangers.

Below: This BAe Strikemaster displays the now-superceded triangular markings worn by South Yemen aircraft. After unification, all Yemini aircraft standardised on the markings of North Yemen.

Yugoslavia

A communist state which yet managed to remain independent of Moscow and outside the Warsaw Pact, Yugoslavia was an artificial country created from several smaller states following the breakup of the Austro-Hungarian Empire in 1919. Held together after World War II by the personality of Marshal Tito, it started to fragment in 1990. Slovenia and Croatia declared independence in 1991, while Bosnia-Herzegovna followed suit early in 1992. Civil war followed, with the dominant Serbian culture trying to dominate the federation states.

The Jugoslovensko Ratno Vazduhoplovsivo (Yugoslav Air Force) has been active in the secessionist wars, although its primary air defence fighter, the MiG-29 Fulcrum, does not appear to have been committed. The MiG-21F/MF Fishbed is numerically the most important type, and these, supported by the indigenous Orao and Jastreb have flown close air support missions, firing pods of unguided rockets. Neither Slovenia nor Croatia have combat aircraft, but light anti-aircraft fire and hand-held SAMs have accounted for several Yugoslav aircraft.

The current YAF insignia is a red star imposed on a white disc with a blue surround, which is carried on the top side of the port wing, the underside of the starboard wing, and the fuselage. The fin flash, a representation of the Yugoslav flag with blue/white/red horizontal bands with a red star central, occupies the complete width of the fin and rudder. The MiG-29s are camouflaged in blue/grey, while the MiG-21s wear light grey all over, or natural metal finish. Oraos and Jastrebs carry green/brown disruptive camouflage. Nose numbers are carried, in red on light grey or aluminium finishes, and in white on camouflage, repeated above the starboard wing.

It seems possible that when the dust has settled, several new air arms will emerge in the newly independent countries. Of these, only Croatia has previously had an air force, when under German occupation during World War II. Croatian markings then were a black/white chequered pattern and this might be revived in the future.

Zaïre

Since 1971 the national flag of Zaïre has featured the blazing torch emblem symbolizing the revolutionary spirit of the nation; it was first used by President Mobutu's Popular Movement of the Revolution established in 1967. Today, the marking is carried on the fin of the surviving Mirage 5M fighter-bombers which equip a single squadron in the Force Aérienne Zaïroise. Although 14 were ordered originally it is believed that no more than nine or ten were actually delivered; of these five or six remain, serialled M401, M402, M403, etc, while three two-seat trainers received were allocated the marking M201, M202 and M203. No fuselage roundels are carried on the Mirages, but they have been seen on the MB.326 light attack aircraft and on other types such as the C-130H Hercules. The latter type also carries the air force title FORCE AERIENNE ZAÏROISE on the forward fuselage and civil registration letters towards the base of the fin (9T-TCA, 9T-TCB, etc). Serials on FAZ aircraft take the form of a role prefix followed by a

number such as FG-462 on an MB.326. As the construction number of this machine was 6462-203, it can be seen that serials are allocated on an internal basis.

Above: The first of three Mirage 5DM trainers in Zaire AF markings. The serial M201 is applied on the rear fuselage as well as on the nosewheel door.

Zambia

The Repubic of Zambia was officially formed in October 1964 and with British assistance established the Zambian Air Force. Initially a transport, liaison and training arm, the

ZAF combat element currently consists of 13 Russian MiG-21MF Fishbeds, 12 Chinese Shenyang F-6s and eight Yugoslav SokoJ-1 Jastrebs. It seems doubtful whether the latter are still serviceable, and more recent Western influence has seen these supplemented by eight Aermacchi MB-326s and SF-260 Warrior armed trainers. The roundel and fin flash are applied in the standard positions, while the serials comprise three-digit numbers in block according to type, prefixed by AF.

Zimbabwe

The combat element of the Air Force of Zimbabwe currently consists of 22 Chengdu F-7M Airguard interceptors, supplemented by eight Hawker Hunter FGA.9s, all of which are operated by No 1 Squadron at Gwelo. Seven remaining BAe Hawk 60s and a dozen SF.260TPs, known locally as

Genets, form No 2 Squadron, flying COIN missions from the same base. Also at Gwelo is No 6 Squadron, equipped with SF.260Cs, which can also carry light armament. New Sarum holds No 6 Squadron, which flies Reims-Cessna FTB.336s, known locally as Lynxes, in the COIN role, while about 20 Alouette IIIs of No 7 Squadron represent the rotary wing combat element.

Four digit serials have been seen, but the Hawks carry three numbers, i.e. 600, 601 etc, in black on the rear fuselage. They are normally camouflaged in tan and olive brown with pale grey undersides.

Combat Camouflage

Camouflage is defined as 'disguise (of aircraft) effected by obscuring outline with splashes of various colours' and the colours applied to modern combat aircraft form an integral part of the machine's basic role. Although there are only seven colours in the spectrum, the camouflaging of aircraft involves all shades, with research and experimentation highlighting some as being more effective than others. As well as concealing and deceiving, colours also reflect the prevailing tensions arising from international relations around the world. Bright colours are often a sign of *détente,* while the application of drab camouflage on front-line aircraft may equally be an indication of a deterioration in one nation's relations with another country or countries.

In most cases modern camouflage is the result of extensive research by scientists using the very latest techniques in paint technology and application. Aircraft are painted and flown in the environment, be it over land or sea, at high or low level, for which the camouflage is designed. Results are analyzed, and orders are issued for the most effective scheme to be applied to the operational aircraft, either by the manufacturer when new-build aircraft are sprayed prior to delivery or at Service maintenance units when machines return for overhaul and a respray in the new colour or colours.

The visibility of an object, be it an aircraft or a tank, depends on its difference in colour and luminance or brightness from its background; luminance is the more important, as

Air superiority

Air defence is one area where a certain commonality exists when it comes to colours. In Western air forces, grey in various shades has been generally accepted as the most effective colour for fighter aircraft. Credit for much of the original research into the new air defence colours must go to the Defensive Weapons Department at the United Kingdom's Royal Aircraft Establishment, Farnborough. In conjunction with British Aerospace, the RAE conducted a series of experiments in the mid-1970s with a specially painted Hunter aircraft which proved that a machine painted overall matt light grey was more difficult to see against the sky than one with a multi-coloured disruptive scheme.

One problem noted by observers during the trials was that some areas of the airframe reflected more than others, while some were darker and throwing distinctive shadows. It was therefore decided to use more than one shade of grey on the aircraft, a lighter shade to brighten the darker areas and a darker shade to tone down the lighter areas, thus giving a uniformity of colour over the whole aircraft — a technique which became known as countershading.

The RAF Phantom force became the first to adopt this new scheme when the aircraft's role changed from offensive support to air defence. Tasked by the RAF's Central Tactics and Trials Organisation, the RAE formulated a subtle combination of Light Aircraft Grey (BS381C-627) for the undersurfaces with Medium Sea Grey (BS381C-637) on the top surfaces and Barley Grey (BS4800-18B21) on the outer wing panels. The result was

colours become less definite with increasing range due to the scattering of light by the atmosphere. The task of the camouflage specialist is to match as closely as possible an aircraft's colour and reflectance with those of its background, no easy task given that a fast-moving aircraft may have a terrain background one minute and a sky background immediately afterwards. Changing weather conditions can also alter the target and background quite considerably and quickly. Therefore, any

Above: Camouflaged Phantoms of 92 Sqn, RAF, formate with a lone grey example illustrating the effectiveness of the lighter colours for fighter operations.

camouflage applied to an aircraft must be a compromise and dependent mainly upon background priority. To illustrate the problems associated with colouring aircraft, this chapter is divided into the individual roles of current combat aircraft.

RAF Tornado F.3

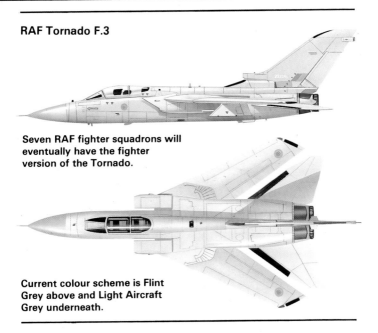

Seven RAF fighter squadrons will eventually have the fighter version of the Tornado.

Current colour scheme is Flint Grey above and Light Aircraft Grey underneath.

dramatic: during mock combat aircrew experienced extreme difficulty in finding the aircraft, particularly at high level.

In 1979 the RAF officially adopted the new scheme for the Phantom and later, in slightly modified form, it was applied to the Lightning and Tornado interceptors. In order not to compromise the whole effect, the mass of external stencilling on the aircraft was reduced (on the Phantom this involved eliminating some 600 servicing instructions of 700 originally carried), white remained absent from the insignia and pastel shades were substituted for the previously bright red and blue colours. A reduction in the size of the main markings was also introduced.

However, despite tactical requirements, RAF fighters continue to operate with squadron badges and markings prominently displayed on tails and fuselages. Applied in bright colours, these form an important part of the Service's *esprit de corps*, but they do little to aid the painstaking efforts of the camouflage specialists. At times of crisis they would be removed, along with all the other markings which an enemy might use to gain a visual advantage in close air combat.

More recently, RAF Hawk T.1As assigned to the point defence role have begun adopting a scheme of Medium Sea Grey over the top surfaces and Barley Grey underneath; again; markings are small and few in number. During the trials which led to the adoption of this scheme, a black dummy canopy was painted on the underside of the forward fuselage to add to confusion in combat. The effectiveness of this device was such that in mock combat flying became extremely hazardous, as pilots were unable to tell which way up the Hawk with the false canopy was. With safety compromised the marking was painted out, but it remains an effective tactical option should the need ever arise.

US approach

The American approach to modern fighter camouflage has followed similar lines. With a new range of advanced combat aircraft under development, both the US Air Force and the US Navy undertook trials in the early 1970s to determine the best colours for the fighter role. Air Superiority Blue was one colour that was much favoured by the USAF in early research, and prototype F-15s and F-16s appeared in this attractive colour. However, it was not adopted: instead, American research came to the same conclusion as the RAE. Grey was the common factor and the McDonnell Douglas and General Dynamics paint shops at St Louis and Fort Worth respectively received instructions to apply shades of grey in carefully formulated schemes to new production F-15s and F-16s.

On the F-15, a countershaded system of two greys (Compass Ghost Greys FS595a 36375 and 36320) covers the aircraft in the form

Below: USAF F-16s of the South Korea-based 8th TFW pictured during Exercise Team Spirit '85. Colours are Dark Grey (saddle area), Middle Grey (nose and fin) and Underbelly Grey (undersides).

USAF F-15C Eagle

Bitburg, West Germany, is the base for this F-15 Eagle, which carries the standard USAF scheme for this air superiority fighter.

Officially called high and low reflectance grey, the scheme consists of Dark Compass Ghost Grey (FS 36320) and Light Compass Ghost Grey (FS 36375).

Luftwaffe F-4F Phantom

Tactical camouflage on a Luftwaffe F-4F Phantom of JG 74.

The Germans derived the sharp-angled 'splinter' scheme from their aircraft of World War II.

shown in the accompanying illustration. Demarcation lines are relatively easy to see at close range, but in the air the two colours merge to conceal the machine against the background. In June 1978 the USAF selected a three-tone grey scheme for the F-16, comprising Dark Grey on the saddle area, Middle Grey on the nose and fin, and Underbelly Grey on the undersurfaces (FS

36081, 36118 and 36375 respectively), while the semi-gloss black radome on early aircraft gave way to Middle Grey when mock combat confirmed that such a heavily contrasting area totally compromised the whole effect.

This three-tone scheme became the standard General Dynamics layout for all F-16s unless customers specified otherwise and some did —

Above: In line with other air forces, the Luftwaffe repainted its F-4Fs in lighter shades of grey, this example being operated by JG 71.

Below: A US Navy F-14A Tomcat about to launch from the USS *Saratoga*. 'Grey on grey' best describes the scheme, the red fin flash providing the only colour.

Norway, for example, requested a single all-over colour, namely Middle Grey, for her aircraft, as they would have to operate over both land and sea and at high and low altitude.

US Naval schemes

The US Navy and Marine Corps tested a number of different schemes before the adoption of three shades of grey in a subtle combination. At one stage, artist Keith Ferris evolved a hard-edged zig-zag pattern of greys for use on the F-14 Tomcat (he produced another for the USAF F-15), but this was aimed at deception rather than concealment and the proposal was not accepted. Codes, national markings and squadron insignia are all applied in subdued form over the standard USN scheme, although some of the famous flamboyant colours associated with the American Navy have crept back into use in a limited fashion, perhaps as a means of rapid identification in the confusion of combat.

Fighters in other countries also changed to lighter camouflage. Dutch F-5s are receiving a countershaded scheme similar to the F-16s,

Swedish Viggen fighters have a light grey in total contrast to the green splinter scheme previously applied, and Federal German F-4F Phantoms are steadily receiving a new combination of no fewer than six colours (RAL7030 Steingrau, 7039 Quartzgrau, 7009 Grüngrau, 7012 Basaltgrau, 7037 Staubgrau and 7035 Lichtgrau).

The French Air Force shunned the application of paint to its interceptors for years, preferring to retain a natural metal finish. However, the arrival of the Mirage F.1 and the new Mirage 2000 highlighted the need for some kind of concealment at altitude — after all, metal gives numerous reflections when unpainted. The result was a blue-grey colour over the upper surfaces, but retaining the natural metal underneath. Mirage 2000s are being delivered to the squadrons in two greys, and a recent modification to the scheme is the overpainting of the black nose radome with light grey to improve overall concealment at high altitude.

Eastern European, Russian and Chinese air arms have traditionally been less innovative than the Western nations in the matter of concealment. Disruptive camouflage was worn mainly by attack and close support aircraft, leaving air superiority fighters in natural metal, or sometimes finished in light grey as a protective rather than a concealment measure. Then with the advent of the new generation MiG-29 Fulcrum and Su-27 Flanker, came a change into two tone blue/grey livery, although in the case of the former, this was not universally adopted by all customer nations.

Paint finishes

As gloss surfaces exhibit glint, which is probably the greatest clue to detection, the ideal paint finish on fighter aircraft, or any combat aircraft for that matter, is matt or, in US parlance, lustreless. However, a major problem with this type of finish is the ease with which it can be contaminated. Aircraft have to be serviced and ground crew need to gain access to parts of the airframe on a regular basis, the result being scuff marks and a quick deterioration of

Above: Sweden experimented with various shades of grey and ended up with the colour seen here. The aircraft is a JaktViggen or fighter JA37 Viggen of the crack F13 Wing based at Norrkoping. On the fin is the unit badge and the engine intake has the FARA or Danger sign prominently displayed. The raked fin tip identifies the JA37 variant.

the surface. Add the occasional spillage of oil and lubricants, and you have an aircraft with the appearance of a 'scrap yard queen' no self-respecting squadron would want to be associated with.

One answer in recent years has been to resort to a semi-gloss finish, which preserves the appearance of the machine but does little for the camouflage requirement; another has been the formulation of a cleaning material which removes all external marks and preserves the vital finish. However, a unit commander should be in no doubt that a scruffy aircraft returning from a mission is better than a smart one that doesn't.

Soviet MiG-31 'Foxhound'

'Blue 21' became the first MiG-31
'Foxhound' to be widely seen by
the West after it was
photographed off northern
Norway in 1985.

The aircraft shows no concession
to individual markings apart from
the large Bort number and the
prominent national insignia.

Ground-attack

The requirements for concealment at low-level are similar to those for air defence: aircraft need colours that match the terrain they fly over or a scheme that will reduce the chances of their being seen by an enemy. Based on disruptive patterns used during the Second World War, RAF front line aircraft were given a scheme of Dark Green/Dark Sea Grey on the upper surfaces and Light Aircraft Grey or Silver undersides from 1953 until the early 1980s. These colours were intended to hide the aircraft on the ground when dispersed around an airfield as well as when flying on operations. The only change to this scheme in recent years has been the elimination of the Light Aircraft Grey and its replacement by the top surface colours wrapped around in pattern form under wings, fuselage and tail. Harriers, Jaguars and Tornados have all been given this form of colouring.

While that old standby grey has proved to be the most adaptable colour for aircraft camouflage, certainly against the sky and, some experts would argue, also against a multicoloured landscape such as the terrain in central Europe, the RAF has decided to adopt a new finish for its Harrier force. This comprises NATO Dark Green in a semi-matt or satin finish over the top surfaces and Litchen Green (BS4800-12B25) on the undersurfaces. The Jaguars and Tornado strike aircraft retain their two-colour coverage.

Right: The F-117A fights exclusively at night, hence the all black finish.

Below: RAF Harrier GR.5s and GR.7s are painted in a two-tone green scheme.

USAF attack aircraft changed from their natural metal finish of the 1950s and early 1960s to the Southeast Asia camouflage of two greens and tan with America's increasing involvement in the Vietnam war. The withdrawal from SE Asia and the US commitment to Europe meant the reassignment of aircraft to bases in West Germany and the UK with the result that it was decided to evolve paint schemes more in keeping with the central European theatre.

European One

One type with a vested interest in low-level survival is the Fairchild A-10 Thunderbolt close-support aircraft. Capable of carrying up to 7 tons of external ordnance and designed to fly round trees instead of over them, the A-10 was used in trials to determine an optimum colour scheme for European-based units. After much experimentation, the result was a disruptive pattern applied over the whole aircraft of Dark Olive Green, Dark Green and Dark Grey (FS 34103, 34092 and 36081 respectively) which was unofficially dubbed 'lizard' but is properly the European One scheme. There appear to be variations to this very dark scheme with FS 36118 replacing 36081 on some aircraft and the grey

USAF A-10 Thunderbolt

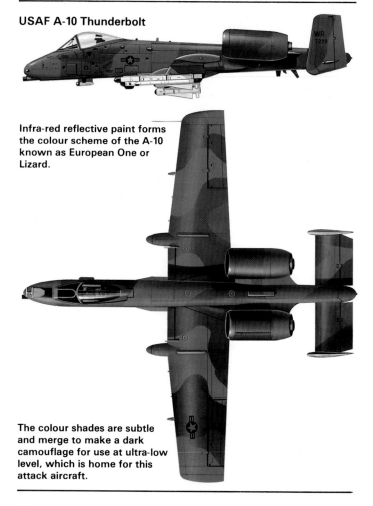

Infra-red reflective paint forms the colour scheme of the A-10 known as European One or Lizard.

The colour shades are subtle and merge to make a dark camouflage for use at ultra-low level, which is home for this attack aircraft.

changing in shade to present what often looks like a different camouflage altogether. Transports like the Lockheed C-5A/B Galaxy and C-141 Starlifter have also received the modified European One scheme, a costly and time-consuming operation, and it is no surprise to learn that the USAF is now considering a change for these aircraft to a more practical and less complicated scheme. It should also be noted that although there is an official three-colour pattern for each aircraft, changes occur from one machine to another.

Below: The SE Asia camouflage pattern wraps round the whole aircraft, as shown on this two-seat A-7K of the 162nd TFG, US ANG, based at Tucson, Arizona.

Luftwaffe Tornado

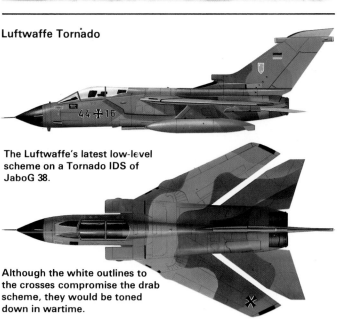

The Luftwaffe's latest low-level scheme on a Tornado IDS of JaboG 38.

Although the white outlines to the crosses compromise the drab scheme, they would be toned down in wartime.

Luftwaffe Alpha Jet

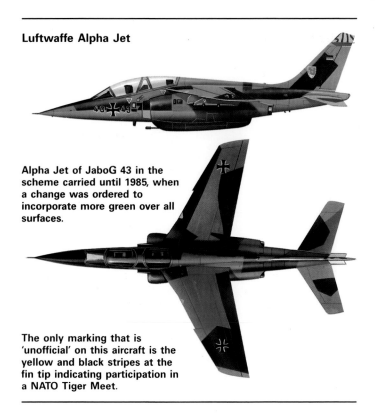

Alpha Jet of JaboG 43 in the scheme carried until 1985, when a change was ordered to incorporate more green over all surfaces.

The only marking that is 'unofficial' on this aircraft is the yellow and black stripes at the fin tip indicating participation in a NATO Tiger Meet.

West Germany's main attack aircraft is the Panavia Tornado, which replaced the F-104G Starfighter, and early aircraft from the Panavia production line were given a disruptive colour scheme of Black, Yellow-olive (RAL6014) and Basalt Grey (RAL7012) over the top surfaces plus Silver Grey (RAL7001) on the lower surfaces. While this was generally in keeping with the usual dark colours employed by most air arms, the Luftwaffe decided that a finish incorporating more green was required. The result was a scheme not unlike the American European One combination and formed of an overall 'wraparound' camouflage of Dark Grey, Dark Green and Medium Green, with the black radome being retained. Luftwaffe Tornados are operated in the counter-air, anti-armour and strike roles, as are the examples flown by the Italian Air Force. The latter have a disruptive pattern of NATO Dark Green (BS381C-641) and NATO Dark Grey (638) over the top surface and Silver on all lower surfaces.

Conflicting requirements

From the foregoing, it is plain that there is no conformity when it comes to aircraft colour schemes. Even NATO with all its STANAGs (Standard Agreements) has not managed to formulate a basic camouflage pattern or even a directive to member nations that their aircraft should adopt certain colours, and while there certainly are NATO colours, they are not used by all the alliance's air arms. Conspiring against the much sought after standardization are the often very different requirements each nation has for its aircraft. Some have a purely overland role, but the dense forests of northern Europe are quite different from the mountainous terrain in Greece and Turkey. For the dual-role mission involving intercept and ground-attack, a compromise colour scheme will be sought, while overwater flying demands an altogether

Soviet Mi-24 'Hind-D'

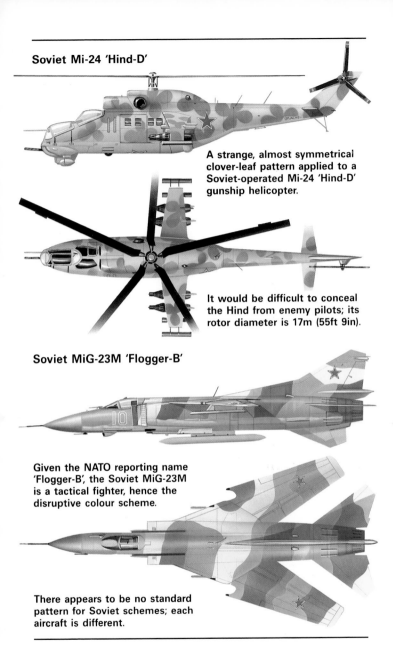

A strange, almost symmetrical clover-leaf pattern applied to a Soviet-operated Mi-24 'Hind-D' gunship helicopter.

It would be difficult to conceal the Hind from enemy pilots; its rotor diameter is 17m (55ft 9in).

Soviet MiG-23M 'Flogger-B'

Given the NATO reporting name 'Flogger-B', the Soviet MiG-23M is a tactical fighter, hence the disruptive colour scheme.

There appears to be no standard pattern for Soviet schemes; each aircraft is different.

different approach to the problem.

Over the border in the East, the numerous ground-attack regiments which formed a large proportion of the former Warsaw Pact air forces had standardized on aircraft types if not on colour schemes. MiG-21s, -23s and -27s, along with Sukhoi Su-17s and a few Su-25s, constituted the vast majority of the attack force, and almost all employ multi-coloured camouflage schemes made up of dark greens, browns, greys and tans.

Precisely how these colours were arrived at will probably never be known for sure. They have a similarity with the American Southeast Asia schemes, but whereas there was some uniformity in those, the Soviet Union and Warsaw Pact seem to have no basic pattern, though matching between aircraft does sometimes occur. The undersurface colour is usually centred on light blue or light grey, the demarcation line being either wavy or straight.

Soviet combat aircraft destined for export to overseas air forces are sprayed in camouflage before despatch. Libyan and Indian MiG-23s have very similar colours, as do the Mil Mi-24/25 attack helicopters flown by the Afghan and Algerian air arms; those supplied to Nicaragua, however, have a predominantly green disruptive scheme for operations over the jungle.

Desert colours

Middle East air forces have traditionally employed a desert finish which during World War II was generally called 'sand and stone' when applied to Allied Spitfires, P-40s, Hurricanes and other types. The Luftwaffe sprayed its Bf 109s and Bf 110s brown over the top surfaces with light blue underneath. Variations on this ranged from large splotches of dark brown or green over the base colour to mottled green

as the North African war drew to a close in the more verdant terrain of Tunisia.

Nowadays, countries like Israel retain desert camouflage for their attack aircraft while grey schemes are used by the interceptors. Kfirs, A-4 Skyhawks and F-4 Phantoms of the Heyl Ha'Avir carry patterns made up of sand, tan and medium green with

Sultan of Oman's Air Force Jaguar

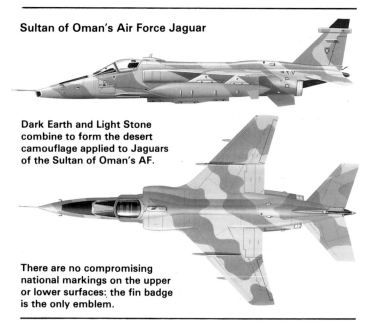

Dark Earth and Light Stone combine to form the desert camouflage applied to Jaguars of the Sultan of Oman's AF.

There are no compromising national markings on the upper or lower surfaces: the fin badge is the only emblem.

pale blue undersurfaces, a combination jokingly referred to as 'Cafe au lait'. Often compromised by large black and orange ID triangles (on the Kfirs), the camouflage proves effective for low-level concealment as well as breaking up the aircraft outline on the ground at airfield dispersals. Further west, Egyptian aircraft are painted in a number of different

Above: Japan received 14 RF-4EJ reconnaissance Phantoms. This example carries one of the early three-tone colour schemes.

finishes, from an overall sand colour to quite dark schemes on the large fleet of MiG-21s; green, tan and brown are, again, common top surface colours.

Heyl Ha'Avir Kfir-C7

Israeli Kfirs assigned the intercept role carry a grey scheme as seen here on aircraft 824.

The aircraft's Mirage III ancestry can be recognized from the plan view, although the foreplanes are innovative additions.

In the Far East, there are few startlingly different colours to relieve the predictability on the camouflage scene. Japanese attack aircraft such as the Mitsubishi F.1 wear a three-colour scheme of mid-green, grey and sand, with grey on the under-surfaces. Their air superiority fighters use a gloss grey on the F-4s but the US two-tone grey scheme on the F-15s. Chinese A-5s have also been seen in a scheme of two greens over a deep blue underside, although most Chinese machines remain unpainted. RAAF F-111s have the US Southeast Asia finish of two greens (FS 34079 and 34102) and tan (30219) with black (37038) undersides. The most modern fighter in the Australian inventory is the licence-built F/A-18 Hornet. In a departure from the dark grey/olive drab disruptive finish of the now withdrawn Mirages, the RAAF has preferred to retain the grey finish currently being applied by McDonnell Douglas to US Navy aircraft. Interestingly enough, each Hornet is given a total of 70 litres of paint — 38 litres sprayed on the undersurfaces and 32 on the top. The matt grey is applied in two coats, with two extra coats on the leading edges, and together with the application of

Above: RAF GR.1 Tornados were tasked with low-level penetration missions during the 1991 Gulf War, and were temporarily painted in an overall 'desert pink' finish. Note the black radome. This example carries the TIALD sensor pod.

markings and insignia the painting takes some ten expensive days on every single aircraft.

Chinese colours

The Chinese Air Force, one of the world's largest, has used dark green as the standard finish for tactical aircraft for many years, although this practice now seems confined to helicopters and trainers. As outlined in the previous section, Chinese combat types are often unpainted, though in recent times ground-attack machines have been noted in a diagonally-striped scheme of green and brown with light blue underneath. This was first seen on A-5 Fantans during the brief war with Vietnam in 1979 and was presumably evolved for operations over the border area between the two countries, but similar schemes have been seen since.

Penetration

Long-range, low-level penetration of an enemy's defences is the task of a select few specialized types. Equipped with the latest electronics to defeat and confuse high-powered early-warning radars and carrying the most lethal and destructive weaponry, these machines constitute one of the biggest threats faced by defensive forces, but such is the very high cost of developing and operating this type of aircraft that they are on the inventories of only a few nations.

Officially the Royal Air Force's strategic bomber, Tornado GR.1 is actually a deep interdiction/strike aircraft, which during the final years of the Warsaw Pact, was the primary British counter-air weapon. Based on airfields in the UK and Germany, they carry both active and passive ECM but also rely on disruptive camouflage for visual concealment. Colours are matt Dark Green (BS381C-641) and Dark Sea Grey (638) over the whole aircraft apart from the radome, which is black. At their peak, eleven Tornado squadrons were operational, two among them being also tasked for the reconnaissance role.

Also based in Europe, although scheduled to be withdrawn by late 1992, are two USAF Tactical Fighter Wings equipped with F-111E and F versions of the early F-111As which saw service in Vietnam. The matt black undersurface colour first applied in Southeast Asia for night attacks has been retained, as has the uppersurface camouflage of two greens and a tan which formed the SE Asia scheme. From 1990, repainting the entire F-111 fleet No. 36118 grey overall has been in hand.

Prior to 1990, the only deviant from the standard F-111 colour scheme was the EF-111A Raven electronic warfare machine, identified by the prominent fin tip pod and the long canoe-shaped radome under the fuselage. These aircraft have a two-grey scheme compatible with their medium- to high-altitude operation, although they are also designed to accompany deep penetration strike aircraft to high-priority targets well inside enemy territory.

The Soviet equivalent of the F-111 is the Sukhoi Su-24. Like its American counterpart it has two crewmen, two engines and swing wings, but it is smaller, lighter and somewhat less capable. However, many hundreds of these low-level attack bombers form the Air Force's tactical 'punch'.

Below: An air defence Hawk of the RAF formates with a Tornado of 617 Sqn displaying its current low-level camouflage colours.

Above: B-52s in 1991 flew in a dark grey/green disruptive pattern, although it often looks like one dark green colour.

Below: The Australians adopted a three tone scheme similar to the US 'South-east Asia' pattern for their F-111Cs.

Inundated with Fulcrums and Flankers as the West has been in recent years, Su-24 Fencers have so far been relatively elusive, but those seen have medium grey upper surfaces with light grey underneath.

The best kept secret was the Lockheed F-117A, revealed in 1989 after years of service. This angular aircraft was designed for low observability in both the radar and infrared spectra. Intended solely for night operations, it is painted matt black all over in radar absorbent paint.

Only the United States and the Commonwealth of Independent States possess truly long range strategic bombers. The USAF has 96 Rockwell B-1B Lancers, which are finished in European One for low level penetration, although during 1991, repainted in overall grey 36118 began. One presumes that this indicates that its future role is seen mainly at medium and high altitudes.

Currently in the flight test stage is the Northrop B-2 of flying wing configuration. This very advanced aircraft is a further generation on in stealth from the F-117A, and is intended to penetrate enemy air defence systems at medium/high altitudes. Finished in mid-grey all over, the B-2 is primarily camouflaged against radar and infra-red, rather than visual detection.

The basic camouflage scheme applied to the enormous Boeing B-52s dated back to the 1960s and consisted of white noses and undersides, with a disruptive pattern of 36081 grey, 34079 and 34159 greens, and 34201 tan. This was amended in the late '80s to 36118 and 36081 grey with 340896 green. This was abandoned in 1988 in favour of all over 36081 grey, modified to the lighter 36118 grey in 1990. It will be some considerable time before all B-52s are standardised on the latest colour.

The CIS Force has done little to camouflage its long-range bomber force and electronics aircraft. Most of the Tu-95 and Tu-142 Bears seen around NATO countries are finished in the natural metal they were built in except for some Naval-operated examples which have a two-tone grey finish divided by a straight line along the sides of the

fuselage. Tupolev Tu-2M 'Backfires' and Tu-16 'Badgers' often appear in grey colours, but these are normally Naval machines rather than Air Force.

France's *Force de Frappe* strategic bomber fleet of Mirage IVs were given disruptive camouflage for the low-level nuclear attack role. Green and grey are the colours used and smaller roundels have been applied to the fuselage and wings

CIS Su-24 'Fencer-C

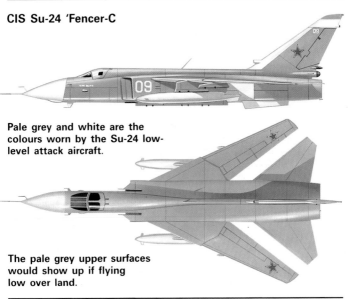

Pale grey and white are the colours worn by the Su-24 low-level attack aircraft.

The pale grey upper surfaces would show up if flying low over land.

CIS Tu-22M 'Backfire'

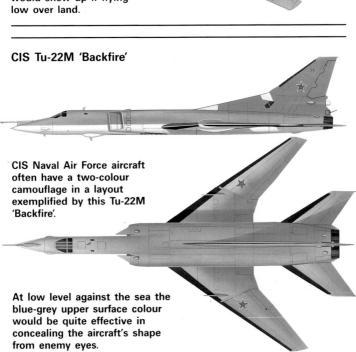

CIS Naval Air Force aircraft often have a two-colour camouflage in a layout exemplified by this Tu-22M 'Backfire'.

At low level against the sea the blue-grey upper surface colour would be quite effective in concealing the aircraft's shape from enemy eyes.

Naval colours

Over-water operations have traditionally dictated certain colours for naval aircraft. These range mainly between light grey and dark blue, though a brief look back at history will show that green has been used in the past, particularly during World War II. Luftwaffe Ju 88s flying in the anti-shipping role carried a 'wave mirror' scheme of light blue snaking lines applied over the basic two-green splinter camouflage, although it is difficult to determine how effective this was in concealing the aircraft from those they were attacking.

South Atlantic experience

For the Royal Navy's Fleet Air Arm, the 1982 South Atlantic War was a milestone in a number of ways, including the noticeable change in the camouflage and markings carried by its aircraft. The withdrawal of the FAA's fixed-wing aircraft element (Phantoms, Buccaneers, Sea Vixens and Gannets) was occasioned by the retirement of the Navy's last conventional carrier, HMS *Ark Royal*, in 1979. However, the fixed-wing aspect did not disappear as in the

same year the FAA accepted the first of its STOVL Sea Harriers. These were finished in the long-established scheme of semi-gloss Dark Sea Grey (BS381C-638) over all upper surfaces and gloss white underneath, while roundels were the conventional red, white and blue and prominent unit insignia decorated the fin.

Then, in 1982, came the brief but hard-fought war with Argentina over the Falkland Islands. The Sea Harrier was the only tactical fighter available to the British Task Force, and 20 aircraft, resplendent in the colours outlined above, sailed aboard the ski-jump-equipped carriers *Hermes* and *Invincible* on April 5, 1982. During their transit south the aircraft were toned down, with the white undersurfaces being given a coat of gloss Extra Dark Sea Grey, the white in the roundels overpainted in blue, and crew names and unit insignia being painted out altogether. Later aircraft ferried out from the UK were finished in semi-matt Medium Sea Grey (BS381C-637) over the top surfaces and fuselage, with semi-matt Barley Grey (BS4800-18B21) on the wing

Royal Navy Fleet Air Arm Sea Harrier FRS.1

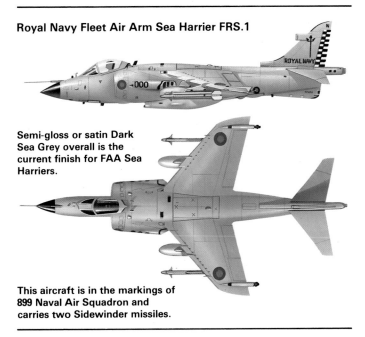

Semi-gloss or satin Dark Sea Grey overall is the current finish for FAA Sea Harriers.

This aircraft is in the markings of 899 Naval Air Squadron and carries two Sidewinder missiles.

and tailplane undersurfaces. Non-essential airframe stencilling was removed and pastel shades of blue and red formed the roundel colours.

Sea Harrier colours

The Sea Harriers suffered no losses in combat with Argentine Mirages and Skyhawks, but aircrew comments about the varied grey schemes used during the war centred on the fact that the best scheme for future use would be a compromise between the Extra Dark Sea Grey and the Medium Sea Grey. Lighter shades than these would certainly compromise aircraft flying over the sea when viewed from above, as Argentinian Navy Skyhawk pilots found to their costs — Light Gull Grey was their usual scheme — and since the war the Sea Harrier force has standardised on an overall satin or semi-gloss Dark Sea Grey colour which may not meet all the pilot's requirements but is probably an acceptable scheme for peacetime flying.

Biggest of all the naval air forces currently in existence is that of the United States, with over 1,800 combat aircraft in service. By tradition,

the US Navy and Marine Corps have consistently maintained highly decorated aircraft, units often vying with each other to produce the brightest and most flamboyant style of tail and fuselage insignia. Basic airframe colours (it would be a misnomer to call it camouflage) have been centred around the liberal use of gloss Light Gull Grey (FS 16440) over most surfaces although gloss white was a standard undersurface colour for many years on US Navy aircraft.

In 1981, however, the USN adopted and began implementing new toned-down camouflage schemes for its front-line fleet similar to those used by the USAF. The F-14 Tomcat, as the Navy's main interceptor, was given an official scheme of dark grey-blue (FS 35237) over the top surfaces, a medium grey (FS 36320) on the side of the fuselage and fins, and light grey (FS 36375) on the undersurfaces, while a similar arrangement is applied to the F-4J Phantoms and A-7E Corsairs. Markings have had the bright colours deleted and national insignia is in outline only. Deterioration is one of

US Navy F/A-18 Hornet

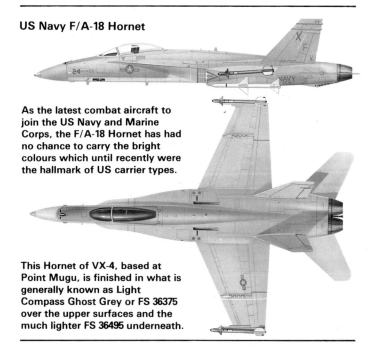

As the latest combat aircraft to join the US Navy and Marine Corps, the F/A-18 Hornet has had no chance to carry the bright colours which until recently were the hallmark of US carrier types.

This Hornet of VX-4, based at Point Mugu, is finished in what is generally known as Light Compass Ghost Grey or FS 36375 over the upper surfaces and the much lighter FS 36495 underneath.

the biggest problems of these matt or lustreless colours and such is the exposure of these schemes to the elements that it is often difficult to determine where the colours change. To prevent unnecessary scuffing of the surfaces maintenance crews are encouraged to wear protective footwear.

Although possessing no carriers, the German Bundesmarine provides NATO with an extra combat force, its Tornado strike and Atlantic patrol aircraft being assigned to cover the Baltic and its environs. Standard Bundesmarine colours for these two aircraft and the Sea King and Lynx helicopters in use are Basalt Grey (RAL7012) over the top surfaces and Light Grey (RAL7035) on the undersurfaces.

Below: A new disruptive camouflage pattern of light and dark greys on a German Navy Tornado of MFG-1.

Bundesmarine Tornado

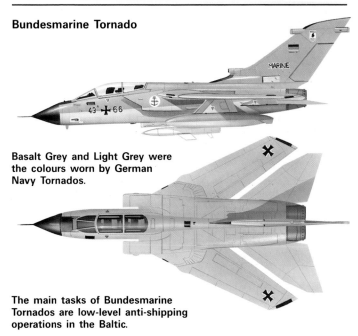

Basalt Grey and Light Grey were the colours worn by German Navy Tornados.

The main tasks of Bundesmarine Tornados are low-level anti-shipping operations in the Baltic.

Above: Two Spanish Navy AV-8A Matadors. No 3 appears to have a replacement rudder.

On the Tornados the fuselage dividing line between the two colours ran along the mid-point, but the high visibility at distance of such a light surface prompted adoption of a random disruptive scheme of multiple-shade greys. Known as the Alberich scheme, this proposal has recently been accepted and will be progressively applied to the fleet. Hand-in-hand with this scheme was to be the general toning down of colour over the airframe, but the markings have been retained in full colour.

The French Navy has two carriers in service, *Clemenceau* and *Foch*, and from these and its shore bases the Aéronavale operates a number of fixed-wing aircraft and helicopters. The premier combat type is the Dassault-Breguet Super Etendard, 71 having been procured by the Service for the strike-attack role. These were delivered in blue-grey and light grey colours, but experience in brief operations over the Lebanon in 1983-84 revealed the need for a more effective camouflage. The result is the application of a disruptive pattern of two greys over the top surface, the lighter shade extending over the undersurfaces.

The CIS Navy has four aircraft carriers, each equipped with a complement of Yak-38 V/STOL fighters and Kamov Ka-25 and Ka-27 helicopters. Painted blue-grey, the Yak-38s have shown no changes to the standard colour scheme since they were first deployed. Howevere, the Su-27 Flanker and MiG-29 Fulcrum used for deck trials on their new fleet carrier wore standard blue/grey air superiority camouflage, and this may well be retained when carrier fighter units are formed.

CIS Yak-38 'Forger'

The Yak-38 'Forger', the Soviet Navy's first fixed-wing carrier-based combat aircraft, operates from Kiev-class ships.

All the Forgers in service have the same basic dark blue-grey colour scheme.

Special colours

Just as nature provides certain creatures with particular colours for protection and concealment from their enemies, so too do the camouflage specialists devise occasional one-off paint schemes for aircraft with special tasks. Sometimes, too, officialdom takes a back seat and units will decide themselves that in order to survive in a particular environment they need their machines finished in a certain way. Usually this originates with personal experience on the part of aircrew who might have survived being bounced by 'enemy' forces during exercises due to flying an aircraft painted in a totally unsuitable colour.

Snow schemes

One example is the finish applied to RAF Harriers and Jaguars, which form part of the UK's commitment to the defence of Northern Norway, during the winter period when a number of NATO exercises are held. The Harriers of 1 Sqn started it with a random coat of whitewash over the top surfaces, leaving the basic dark green-grey camouflage showing through to help break up the outline. Later, 41 Sqn went one better and devised a light blue and white scheme, again using a washable distemper, for their Jaguars. More recently the Jaguars have received large patches of white over their dark green-grey, reminiscent of the random schemes applied to Luftwaffe Bf 109s and He 111 bombers operating in this area during the 1939-45 war. One drawback with this temporary colouring is the appalling finish which results from a few days' intensive operations, but this is deemed a small penalty to pay when the camouflage is instrumental in enabling the aircraft to successfully complete their missions.

Below: An experimental winter scheme of white applied over the basic green/grey colours of a Jaguar of 41 Sqn, RAF, makes it almost invisible against a Norwegian mountainside.

What do you do when an aircraft the size of a four-jet Nimrod requires a new camouflage scheme? Such a question was posed to camouflage specialist Philip Barley at RAE Farnborough in the mid-1970s. Since the introduction of the Nimrod maritime patrol aircraft, it had operated in a finish of gloss white on top and light grey underneath, and its Achilles heel was the glint which continually bounced off the curved surface of the fuselage and from the cockpit area. A flat surface will normally only glint instantaneously — enough to attract attention but without necessarily continuing to show — but a sustained glint will give the game away completely. A toning down was required, and as the big aircraft spent a considerable time on the ground at open air dispersals, a colour was needed that would closely match concrete.

Concrete camouflage

As a result of colour and reflectance research, Hemp was chosen as the shade that matched concrete most closely, and when an aircraft was painted and flown in comparative trials with a white Nimrod it was found that in almost all air-to-air situations it was better than the old scheme — an example of a scheme geared to an airfield background pro-

Above: With the main intention of camouflaging aircraft against large areas of concrete hardstandings, the RAF's Nimrod MR.2 maritime patrol force was given a scheme of Hemp over the top surfaces and Light Grey underneath. Although the machines on the ground are clearly visible in this view, a potential high speed, low-level attacker could have problems.

ving just as good if not better in the air. So the Nimrod force has been steadily receiving the Hemp and grey camouflage as each aircraft comes up for major servicing, and the RAF has also specified the scheme for the VC10 tanker fleet.

Colour confusion

Sometimes colour schemes go wrong, not just on a single aircraft such as the first Hemp-coloured Nimrod which was finished in dark brown and subsequently had to be repainted, but en masse, as illustrated by the 15 ex-US Navy F-4J Phantoms acquired by the RAF to maintain the strength of UK-based air defences following the deployment of 23 Sqn to the Falklands in 1982. When the re-worked F-4J(UK) Phantoms arrived at their Wattisham base for 74 Sqn, their colours were

Above: An example of how two different air forces tackle the same problem. In the foreground, a USAF KC-10 Extender air refuelling tanker finished in the charcoal colour which has become the standard camouflage for this type of aircraft. On the right is an RAF VC10 tanker which has the Hemp and Light Grey scheme. The Hemp shade approximates to BS2660-4-049.

Below: The black finish over all but the upper surfaces of this MC-130E Hercules of the 7th Special Operations Squadron, USAF, serves two purposes: first to absorb radar signals and second to reduce visual acquisition during the highly classified missions undertaken by this unit. The 7th is based in Germany; other units are based in Florida and the Philippines.

Above: If you can't conceal it — confuse it! This F-16XL prototype was given a shaded diagonal scheme with a false fin shadow, cockpit and refuelling marking on the underside.

Below: Known as rectilinear disruptive camouflage, this scheme was devised by artist Keith Ferris and tested by the US Navy on six F-14A Tomcats during trials in 1977.

USAF Aggressor F-5E

This F-5E Aggressor aircraft was based at RAF Alconbury, UK, and wears the scheme known as 'Frog'. Note the stencilled national insignia and USAF on the wings.

The disruptive schemes applied to Aggressor aircraft were intended to depict colour combinations used by Eastern Bloc air arms, adding realism to training.

noticeably different from those on 56 Sqn FGR.2s. The scheme should have conformed with the standard Phantom colours (Light Aircraft Grey/Medium Sea Grey/Barley Grey) but the semi-matt finish was applied by the US Navy using American colours — Neutral Grey (FS 36170), Barley Grey equivalent (FS 36314) and Gull Grey (FS 36440). The high quality finish was found to be much easier to keep clean than the UK matt finish, but the aircraft were repainted during scheduled maintenance.

Gulf war schemes

The massive allied deployment to the Kuwait theatre of operations in 1990/91 saw some interesting paint jobs emerge. USAF combat aircraft retained their normal schemes, making no concessions to desert operations. With the technical and numerical superiority of the coalition forces, a massive repainting operation was hardly justified. Many USAF aircraft carried lo-viz markings, but on others, bright unit insignia were evident. Experiments with more suitable disruptive desert camouflage for A-10A Thunderbolts were carried out in the USA, but not applied in the Gulf region.

Above: Hardly camouflage, but typical of the gaudy markings often applied for special occasions. This Belgian F-16A was the star attraction at the 1985 NATO Tiger Meet. Specially coloured latex was used, applied over seven coats of primer to protect the aircraft's anti-radar paint. Only one flight was made in these colours as it was found that large areas peeled in the air.

Below: Three anniversaries in one. The RAF painted this F-4 Phantom in 1979 to mark the 60th anniversary of the crossing of the Atlantic by Alcock and Brown in 1919 and also included the 30th anniversary of NATO and Rolls-Royce's 60 years of aero engine production at Derby. It landed at Greenham Common on June 21, having crossed the Atlantic in just over five hours.

The US Navy and Marine Corps also stuck to their normal paint schemes for fixed wing aircraft; as noted earlier, bright unit markings were evident on some aircraft, notably those of USS *America, Independence,* and *John F. Kennedy.* USMC Harrier IIs underwent one immediate change on arrival in the Gulf; the insides of their 'elephant ear' intakes were painted gloss white in order to minimise the 'black hole' effect projected by the AV-8B from head-on.

Helicopters were a rather different matter. Sea Stallions of HMM-463 carried no less than six different colour schemes, ranging from all-over pale grey to all-over olive drab, while USMC Sea- and SuperCobras varied between two-tone pale grey, two-tone desert pink, and spinach and sand disruptive schemes.

The Royal Air Force made considerably more effort towards concealment. Tornado F.3s retained their air superiority finish, but GR.1s, Buccaneers and Jaguars were finished in all-over desert pink, which wear and tear soon reduced to a mucky shade of ochre which was probably-just as effective. National markings were lo-viz, or even omitted altogether in some cases, with two letter codes outlined in white on the

fin. Some helicopters were also finished in this manner, while others sported a pink/black mottle. RN Lynxes retained their normal sea grey finish, but carried a large Union Flag astern of the fuselage door. Victor, VC-10 and Tristar-tankers were finished all-over hemp.

Italian Tornados were painted an all-over sand colour, with small roundels on the fuselage sides ahead of the intakes, no fin flash, and small two digit aircraft numbers at the top of the fin. Many Armee de l'Air aircraft also carried desert camouflage, notably the Jaguar As, some finished in all-over sand and others in disruptive sand and stone, with toned down national markings, and codes in matt black.

Show schemes

Some colours painted on combat aircraft have the totally opposite effect of concealing them. The annual Tiger Meet held by NATO squadrons with a Tiger in their badge has regularly encouraged flamboyant colour schemes. Black and yellow stripes have been painted on a number of different aircraft types including Starfighters, F-16s, Phantoms and even a Puma helicopter, often accompanied by a large tiger's head on the nose. The application of these schemes and others which celebrate anniversaries of units or famous personnel is not always encouraged by officialdom: painting complicated designs on an aircraft can be very time-consuming, and some unit commanders would argue that it also impairs squadron efficiency. An acceptable compromise is often worked out however, such as a coloured tail or a particularly graphic piece of nose art.

With all the research and experimentation expended on finding the correct camouflage for today's modern warplane, perhaps it is sobering to reflect that nature has already sorted out the problem. Birds have colours suitable for their environment and in a sense they have the same fundamental problem — to catch their prey without being seen. Maybe the camouflage experts should take a leaf out of their book — or maybe they already have.

OTHER SUPER-VALUE MILITARY GUIDES IN THIS SERIES

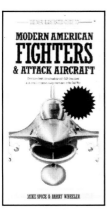

OTHER ILLUSTRATED MILITARY GUIDES AVAILABLE

Modern Tanks & Fighting Vehicles
Modern Rifles & Sub-Machine Guns
Modern Warships
Weapons of the Elite Forces
Modern Elite Forces

★ Each title has 160 fact-filled pages
★ Each is colorfully illustrated with hundreds of action photographs and technical drawings
★ Each contains concisely presented data and accurate descriptions of major international weapons systems
★ Each title represents tremendous value for money